Tantalizing Tidbits for Teens:

Quick Booktalks for the Busy High School Library Media Specialist

By Ruth E. Cox, Ph.D.

A Publication of THE BOOK REPORT & LIBRARY TALK
Professional Growth Series

Linworth Publishing, Inc.
Worthington, Ohio

By
Ruth E. Cox, Ph.D.
University of Houston-Clear Lake
School of Education
2700 Bay Area Blvd.
Houston, TX 77508
281-283-3549
Cox@cl.uh.edu
December 18, 2001

Cataloging-in-Publication Data

Published by Linworth Publishing, Inc.
480 East Wilson Bridge Road, Suite L
Worthington, Ohio 43085

Copyright © 2002 by Linworth Publishing, Inc.

All rights reserved. Reproduction of this book in whole or in part is prohibited without written permission of the author

1-58683-017-1

5 4 3 2 1

Table of Contents

About the Author iii

Dedication iii

1. Introduction 1

2. Annual Recommended Reading Lists 5
      A. The Young Adult Library Services Association (YALSA) Lists 5
      B. The International Reading Association (IRA) Lists 6

3. Awards
      Michael L. Printz Award 7
      Coretta Scott King Award 7
      Pura Belpre Award 8

4. Booktalking Techniques 9

5. Booktalks 13

6. Indexes 121
      A. Author 121
      B. Title 125
      C. Subject 128
      D. Genre 131
      E. Curriculum Connections 131

About the Author

Ruth E. Cox is an Assistant Professor in the School of Education at the University of Houston – Clear Lake, where she teaches courses in Young Adult Literature, Children's Literature and Administration of School Library Media Centers. She previously held school library media positions in Texas, Wisconsin and Alaska. Ruth has been President of the Wisconsin Association of School Librarians, on the BBYA, Printz, Newbery, Carnegie and both AASL and YASLA Intellectual Freedom Committees.

Dedication

To Dr. Betty Carter, my mentor at Texas Woman's University, who nurtured and encouraged my involvement in young adult literatue.

SECTION 1

Introduction

Tantalizing Tidbits for Teens is a tool to help busy high school library media specialists entice teens to slow down for a bit and curl up with a good book, get lost in a mystery, find themselves in a character, or discover new worlds. These short booktalks are meant to be just that—tidbits to tantalize the reader. They give teens the first taste of a delicious book. Like a just-baked cookie, they can't take one bite and stop there.

These tidbits can go anywhere with the library media specialist. A single booktalk can be shared with a student in the hallway, or a planned booktalking session can be done in the classroom, accompanied by a book truck. Within a few minutes, numerous booktalks can be shared and books checked out. Before leaving, the library media specialist lets the students know that more great books are available in the library media center.

Because the audience for *Tantalizing Tidbits for Teens* is high school library media specialists, the novels included are appropriate for grades nine through twelve library media center collections. The information on interest level has been confirmed in review sources such as *Book Report, Booklist, Kirkus Review, School Library Journal,* and *Voice of Youth Advocates (VOYA).* When possible, more than one review source level is included. If the book is an adult book that is on the Best Books for Young Adults list or the Alex Awards list, the level is listed as adult. Fewer than a handful of books did not have current information on interest level readily available.

TANTALIZING TIDBITS FOR TEENS: QUICK BOOKTALKS FOR THE BUSY HIGH SCHOOL LIBRARY MEDIA SPECIALIST
SECTION 1: INTRODUCTION

Since some of these booktalks are on novels intended for older teen readers, they may be considered controversial. To ensure that these novels are appropriate for high school library media centers, a majority of them are on the American Library Association or the International Reading Association recommended reading lists, which target teens. A small number are noted as "Author's Choice." These are novels that have been positively reviewed and are my favorites to booktalk, but have not made the annual lists at the time of publication. Please keep in mind that it is each library media specialist's responsibility to determine which of these titles he or she feels comfortable booktalking. Always read a book before booktalking it.

Each entry in *Tantalizing Tidbits for Teens* includes an annotation because the library media specialist selecting novels to booktalk or to add to the collection needs more information about the plot, characters, and setting than a booktalk can give. Booktalks are meant to entice, not to tell the whole story. The age of the main character is included whenever possible, but keep in mind that the age of a protagonist does not always match the age of the intended reader. For example, *This Is GraceAnne's Book* (St. Martin's Press, 1999) is a novel marketed for the adult reader, but has teen appeal because of the issues the young protagonists experience, not the ages of the characters. The main character, GraceAnne, is twelve, and her nine-year-old brother, Charlie, narrates the story. Therefore, while creating a booktalk, I rarely ever mention the age of the protagonist.

Each entry also includes purchasing information for editions that are in print, hardback or paperback. Some library media specialists prefer hardbacks, but others opt to buy several paperback copies of popular titles for their collections. If the entry does not include information for a paperback edition, the library media specialist can check the availability of both formats through *Books in Print*, as well as on the Web sites of Amazon, <www.amazon.com> and Barnes and Noble, <www.barnesandnoble.com>; a paperback edition may have been published since *Tantalizing Tidbits for Teens* went to press. A number of the titles included are available only in paperback edition at this time. It is not unusual for a popular young adult title to no longer be available in hardback, but to stay in paperback print for many years, with numerous reprints and new cover art. Lois Duncan's *I Know What You Did Last Summer* (Laurel Leaf, 1999) is an excellent example of a paperback edition with new cover art that appeals to teen readers. The newest cover is a photograph of the young actors and actresses in the movie by the same name, which is loosely based on the novel.

Each entry includes a subject listing. These lists are not Library of Congress subject headings in all cases, but rather subjects requested by teachers or by teen readers. For example, the psychology teacher may ask for a booktalking session on novels addressing issues such as mental illness, pregnancy, and suicide. A subject index is included.

Curriculum connections are included to help the library media specialist match titles to teacher requests. Many entries include an activity related to the curriculum or ways to integrate the book and others like it into the classroom curriculum. Although curriculum areas are listed, the activities also may be relevant to other curriculum areas. Many of the activities include a research element to ensure involvement with the library media center. The activities also encourage team teaching by the classroom teacher and the library media specialist. An index of the curriculum areas is included.

Along with subject and curriculum requests, library media specialists will receive requests for books in a particular genre. Each entry lists the genre or genres. I have not tried to balance the number of novels in relation to different genres. The predominant genre in *Tantalizing Tidbits for Teens* is realistic fiction, as more of these novels have made the recommended reading lists than any other genre. A number of the "Author's Choice" novels are fantasy or science fiction to round out the variety of genres. A genre index is included.

Each entry includes the abbreviated name of the book list or lists and the year the novel was on the list. A title may be on the Best Books for Young Adults list, the Quick Picks for Reluctant Young Adult Readers list, and on a later year's Popular Paperbacks list. In 1994 and 2000, professionals of young adult literature who attended pre-conferences at the American Library Association Annual Conference examined the previous years' Best Books for Young Adults lists and created a Best of Best Books list. These two lists also have been examined for older titles that still have teen appeal and are still in print. In a small number of cases, the books that are on the Young Adult Library Services lists also appear on the Young Adults' Choices list. Titles that I have chosen that are not on a list include the notation "Author's Choice." These titles may have been nominated for one of the lists, are too new to be on a list, or are some of my favorite booktalk titles.

If the novel has received the Printz, Coretta Scott King, or Pura Belpre Award, this is listed in the entry. These awards are given for both children's and young adult books.

Each entry includes the abbreviated name of the review journal(s) and the suggested interest level and grade ranges. Some interest level ranges include grades that are below high school, but they still include grades nine and ten or higher. Please note that reviewer grade level suggestions are just that—suggestions. The suggested interest level ranges among the review journals may vary considerably. If an interest level was not available, this also is noted.

The preceding information is included for each title entry to assist the library media specialist in putting together booktalking sessions of various types. The library media specialist may browse through *Tantalizing Tidbits for Teens* to find booktalks to introduce a wide variety of novels to students or to select titles for curriculum-related booktalking sessions. The author, title, subject, genre, and curriculum connection indexes greatly enhance the usability of this book.

Integrating literature into the curriculum and helping create lifelong readers are part of what proactive library media specialists do on a daily basis. *Tantalizing Tidbits for Teens* is a resource for library media specialists and teachers to accomplish those goals.

Annual Recommended Reading Lists

Thousands of novels are published for teens each year in the United States. Professional journals, such as *Book Report, Booklist, Kirkus, School Library Journal*, and *Voice of Youth Advocates (VOYA)*, include reviews of many new young adult titles. However, there is no guarantee that the novels the reviewers are recommending are the ones teens are selecting. To touch both bases—the recommendations of the professionals and the choices of teen readers—a majority of the titles selected for inclusion in *Tantalizing Tidbits for Teens* is found on the lists described on pages 5-6. The entries also include novels that appear on the 1994 and 2000 Best of the Best Books for Young Adults lists that were compiled from annual lists from prior years.

A. The Young Adult Library Services Association (YALSA) Lists

The titles on the Alex Awards, Best Books for Young Adults, the Popular Paperbacks, and the Quick Picks for Reluctant Young Adult Readers lists are chosen by committees of professionals in the area of young adult literature. These professionals are members of the Young Adult Library Services Association (YALSA), a division of the American Library Association (ALA). Although informational books, poetry collections, and short story collections appear on these lists, the booktalks in *Tantalizing Tidbits for Teens* are only on novels included on the 1995–2002 lists. Titles with publication dates prior to 1995 will appear, however, because the Popular Paperbacks list and the Best of Best Books lists include older titles. Copies of these lists are available on the Young Adult Library Services Association Web site at <www.ala.org/yalsa>. Additional information about the policies and procedures of the Young Adult Library Services Association committees is available online at <www.ala.org/yalsa/yalsainfo>.

The Alex Awards committee annually chooses a list of 10 adult titles based on literary quality, readability, and strength of teen appeal. The list encompasses a variety of genres that introduce teens to adult books. The titles are chosen from books published in the previous calendar year and marketed primarily to adults.

The Best Books for Young Adults annual list presents books, those marketed both to adults and to young adults, published within the last 16 months that are recommended reading for teens. The committee does not try to balance the list in relation to reading tastes, levels, genres, or subject areas.

The Popular Paperbacks committee annually prepares one to five annotated list(s) of at least 10, but no more than 25, recommended titles selected from popular genres, topics, or themes. The intention of the list is to present teens with a selection of titles representing a broad variety of themes and subjects, readily accessible in paperback format. Committee members decide on the genres, themes, and subjects, with popularity being more important than literary quality. There is no limit on the copyright date of these young adult and adult titles, as long as they are in print in paperback format.

The Quick Picks for Reluctant Young Adult Readers committee prepares an annual annotated list of recommended books published in the last 18 months that are appropriate for reluctant teen readers. These titles are intended for recreational reading, not for remedial or curriculum use. The titles should appeal to teens. The subject matter, cover art, readability, format, and style are considered when nominating and voting on titles.

B. The International Reading Association (IRA) List

Teen readers from around the United States choose the 30 books on the annual Young Adults' Choices list. Each year the International Reading Association selects team leaders from five different regions of the United States. The team leaders then choose several secondary schools within their areas to receive books marketed for young adults. Publishers send books, which have received two positive reviews in recognized review journals, to the team leaders, who then coordinate the placement of these books in the selected schools. The teens select what they want to read, voting on their favorites. The 30 books (fiction or nonfiction) with the most votes become the list, which is then annotated by the members of the Literacy for Young Adults Committee. The results are announced at the International Reading Association National Conference in May. The Young Adults' Choices list is available on the International Reading Association Web site at <www.readingonline/reviews/choices/choicesindex.html>.

Section 3

Awards

A. Michael L. Printz Award

The Michael L. Printz Award is an award for literary excellence in young adult literature. A nine-member selection committee annually names one award and as many as four honor books. The books must be published between January 1 and December 31 of the prior year and be designated as a young adult title by the publisher, or one published for the age range of 12 through 18. The books may be fiction, nonfiction, poetry, or an anthology, and may have been previously published in another country. More information about this award can be found at <www.ala.org/yalsa/printz/aboutaward.html>.

B. Coretta Scott King Award

The Coretta Scott King Task Force of the American Library Association's Social Responsibilities Round Table annually presents the Coretta Scott King Award. The purpose of this award is to encourage the expression of the African-American experience through literature and the graphic arts. The author or illustrator must be African-American, and the book must portray some aspect of the black experience.

A seven-member award jury chooses an annual award for both author and illustrator. The award-winning titles must be written for children or young adults within the three following categories: preschool–grade 4, grades 6–8, and grades

9–12. Because of the final category, some of the novels included in *Tantalizing Tidbits for Teens* are titles that have won the Coretta Scott King Award or are Coretta Scott King honor books. More information about this award can be found at the official Coretta Scott King Web site at <www.ala.org/srrt/csking>.

C. Pura Belpre Award

The Pura Belpre Award is presented biennially to a Latino/Latina writer and illustrator whose work in literature for children or young adults best portrays, affirms, and celebrates the Latino culture. This award is co-sponsored by the Association of Library Services for Children (ALSC), a division of the American Library Association (ALA), and the National Association to Promote Library Services to the Spanish Speaking (REFORMA).

Section 4

Booktalking Techniques

Mike Printz is the high school library media specialist for whom the newly created young adult literature award is named. In a September 1993 interview in *School Library Journal's Best* (Neal-Schuman, 1997), he stated that booktalking to a group of high school students is one of the greatest motivational tools a high school library media specialist has. "Of all the things I've ever done, that would have to be the greatest rush in the world. To be able to talk about books and turn somebody on; to have them come up and almost pull the book out of your hand or knock you over to pick up the book because they want to read." But a lengthy booktalk that "tells it all" will not have teens rushing to get the books, as they did when Printz booktalked to them. He was a pro. He knew how to find an element or event in a book that would relate to teens' lives. Booktalking is as easy as tying one's shoe for some library media specialists and as difficult as doing calculus in one's head for others. The booktalks included in *Tantalizing Tidbits for Teens* are short enough to be memorized by the novice booktalker or to be used as style hints for the pro.

Booktalking is a lot like acting, but in this case the booktalker also is the writer, the producer, and the director. There is no off-scene director shouting, "Cut!" if the booktalker deviates from the "script." Some booktalkers work from outlines or notes, and others have actual "scripts" that they memorize. There is no right or wrong way to prepare for a booktalk, but preparation is a must. It is never wise for a library media specialist to booktalk a book that he or she has not read, or one that he or she cannot recommend. The teen who enjoyed a booktalked novel may want to discuss it with the library media specialist. Having read the book, and similar titles to recommend, ensures that the follow-up discussion is satisfying for both the library media specialist and the teen reader.

Booktalks are as unique as the person presenting them, but three styles of booktalks are most often given. The first style is the easiest: Find a juicy tidbit of text and read it aloud to the students, leaving them with a cliffhanger. The cliffhanger excerpt should have the audience wanting more—they want to know what happens next. When reading, keep page flags available to mark the cliffhanger passages for future booktalks. Remember to write the page(s) down elsewhere, as the book being shared will more than likely be checked out at the conclusion of the booktalk. This style of booktalk is not present in *Tantalizing Tidbits for Teens;* the booktalks in this book were created by its author and do not contain excerpts from the novels.

The second booktalking style takes a bit more work. The booktalker shares tidbits of the plot, setting, character, or an intriguing incident from the book to get teens' attention. The booktalker also may ask the audience a question. For example, a booktalk on the 2000 Printz Award novel, *Monster* (HarperCollins, 1999), by Walter Dean Myers, may start with the simple question: "Is there ever a right time to not tell the truth?" Then the booktalker may lead a short discussion of how people define "truth" in different environments and under different circumstances. The discussion keeps the audience active and opens the door for the booktalker to share the main character's personal redefinition of truth while on trial for murder.

The third booktalking style takes some acting skill. The booktalker becomes one of the characters in the book and talks to the audience about what is happening to him or her. A booktalker might become John, in *Hard Love* (Simon & Schuster, 1999), the Printz Award honor book by Ellen Wittlinger: "It is bad enough that I normally am in neutral when it comes to girls, but then, when I do fall for one, she is a Puerto Rican lesbian with spiky black hair so sharp on the ends you swear they could pierce your heart."

Each booktalker finds his or her unique style with practice, but it is wise to vary the types of booktalks given in a session covering a number of books. If you read excerpts from every book, the audience will get bored. It also is a good idea to move around. Walk about in at least the front of the room, if not among the audience. If notes are necessary, put them on the back of the books. Take care to not hold the book up in front of your face; this can be distracting for the listeners. The audience needs to see the emotion and conviction on your face. Also, remember to remove the notes from the back covers so the teens can check out the books.

If you are preparing to booktalk the first time and are uncomfortable with the process, videotape yourself doing sample booktalks. Specific mannerisms will be evident, as will body movements, which may need to be modified or eliminated. For example, booktalkers who use index cards have been known to tap the index cards against the lectern or table while talking, much to the irritation of the audience, who hears the tapping, not the booktalk. These little things will show up when watching the videotape, as will the number of times "um," "like," and other filler words are used. Be attentive to how and where the book is being held, so the audience can see it. Hold the book so that your hand does not cover the title of the book on the front cover. Make smooth transitions between books, rather than saying "And this book is…" before picking up every book. Avoid saying, "I really liked this book." The audience has already assumed that the book is good. Why else is it being booktalked?

Some booktalkers include "slides" of book covers. This is effective when booktalking to a very large group, but with a smaller group, such as a class of students, holding the book up while talking about it is the most effective means of introducing it to the audience. After sharing each title, stand the book on a table in front of the room and move on to the next book. Although multiple copies of a title being booktalked may be available in the library, including some that are tattered and torn, always use a visually attractive copy for the booktalk. The paperback edition cover art often has more teen appeal than the hardback. Don't hold up a hardback edition with the dust jacket missing; gray or navy covers have no visual appeal. Teens, like readers of any age, often select books because of their covers. If the cover is not appealing, they may never open it to get to the "good stuff" inside.

To ensure that the audience remembers the book, clearly state the author and title before and after the booktalk. So that students can mark the titles they are most interested in reading, hand out a list of the books with catchy, attention-getting one-liners for each title before beginning the booktalking session. Formatting the list as a bookmark may help ensure that potential readers don't toss the list in the trash. Include similar titles on the list, as more than likely there won't be enough copies of the booktalked titles to meet reader demand. If only one copy of a book being booktalked is available, make sure to bring numerous similar titles. This alleviates the frustration that may occur when students get excited about a book, but cannot check it out because of a waiting list. Consider sharing the list of booktalked titles with the public library and the local bookstore so they will be prepared for those readers with public library cards or cash to borrow/or buy the books.

A booktalk's audience and environment will determine the length of the session. A short, informal booktalk with one student may take place in the library media center or even in the school hallway. On the other hand, 30 minutes is a suitable length of time to booktalk to a group of students. Approximately 20 titles can be shared in a 30-minute session, but more books than can be booktalked during the session should be available. You may talk faster than you had planned, or observe during the booktalk, by "reading" your audience, that some of the books are not relevant to this particular group. Allow time for the students to ask questions, to browse through the books, and to check them out.

Logistically, booktalks are usually easier when you go to the classroom rather than the other way around. Many teachers do not have the time to take their students to the library media center. In a large high school, a good portion of the class period may be used to walk to the library media center and to get the students settled down. You can be waiting in the classroom, prepared to start booktalking as soon as the students are seated. The goal is to "advertise" as many of the books in the library media center as possible. Also, visiting the classrooms gives you additional visibility in the school.

With the advent of hand-held barcode scanners, you can check out books in the classroom. If a hand-held scanner is not available, a sign-out sheet with entry points for the student's name, identification number, and the barcode of the book also will work. The information can be entered in the computer later.

At the conclusion of the booktalking session, ask the teacher and students for input. If a particular booktalk did not go over well, it may not have been the book, but rather the content or the style of the booktalk itself. Is there another element of the book that would have made a better booktalk topic? Perhaps the presentation style of the booktalk needs to be changed.

As soon as possible after booktalking and taking into account the audience input, make notes on how the session went and keep the originals of the list for later use. To keep from repeating booktalks with the same group of students, write each session's date and audience on the back of the list or on the booktalk cards. Some booktalkers keep these notes in a computer file, along with the booktalk titles list, so they can be adapted for later use.

Individual booktalks also should be filed for later use. Some booktalkers use three-ring binders with a booktalk per page. Others use index cards and file them in a box. Some create a database for the titles they booktalk and add new booktalks for previously booktalked titles, as well as notes about what worked and didn't work well. Whatever the filing and storage system used, you will compile a wealth of booktalks through the years. These booktalks can be repeated, expanded upon, and in some cases totally changed, based on the listening audience.

Booktalking should be an integral element of the high school library media program. Along with group booktalks, offer to do one or two booktalks during the morning announcements and design a special display for the booktalked books. If the school has a TV studio, offer to do booktalks on the air, as well as assist students in writing and broadcasting their own booktalks for their favorite books.

Use booktalking to highlight the leisure reading element of the library media program that is so often overlooked because of the extensive use of the high school library media center for research projects and curriculum-related assignments. It is the role of the library media specialist to educate students, parents, faculty, and administrators to the fact that helping students become lifelong readers goes hand in hand with teaching information literacy skills.

Booktalks

Abbreviations used in this section:

Alex	Alex Awards (adult books recommended for young adults)
B of BBYA	Best of the Best Books for Young Adults
BBYA	Best Books for Young Adults
BL	*Booklist*
BR	*Book Report*
K	*Kirkus Review*
PP	Popular Paperbacks for Young Adults
QP	Quick Picks for Reluctant Young Adult Readers
SLJ	*School Library Journal*
VOYA	*Voice of Youth Advocates*
YAC	*Young Adults' Choices*

1 Abelove, Joan, *Saying It Out Loud.*

DK Ink, 1999, 136 pp. $15.95. ISBN: 0-7894 2609-9. Penguin Putnam, 2001. 144pp. $5.99. ISBN: 0-1413-1227-0
Subjects: Cancer, Death, Fathers and Daughters, Jewish Americans, Race Relations
Genres: Multicultural, Realistic
List: 2000 BBYA
Levels: BL 7–12, SLJ 8 & Up

Annotation: Sixteen-year-old Mindy's mother is dying of a brain tumor. Her father is so unreachable that she turns for comfort to her best friend, Gail, and to a new boy in school who is not Jewish, even though she is forbidden to date a Gentile.

Booktalk: Why won't he talk to me? Why didn't he tell me what was happening? I know you're in the hospital. You have a brain tumor. On Saturday I talked to you while you sat in your hospital bed, on Monday the doctor told us they removed the tumor and you were resting comfortably. But now almost a week has gone by, it is Friday, and he is just now telling me that you don't even know he's there when he visits you. I have to decide if I want to visit you. Do I want to see you that way? Why didn't he prepare me for this? Mom, I don't know how to deal with this… but you can't help me now, can you?

Curriculum Connection: English

Mindy makes numerous references to children's classics. Have readers locate these references and discuss their relevance to the novel. Ask teen readers if they have read the children's books. Have copies of these books available for students to either revisit or experience for the first time.

2 Alder, Elizabeth, *The King's Shadow.*

Farrar, Straus & Giroux, 1995, 259pp. $17. ISBN: 0-374-34182-6. Dell, 1997, 272pp. $4.50. ISBN: 0-440-22011-4.
Subjects: Kings, Middle Ages, Physically Handicapped, Slavery
Genre: Historical
Lists: 1998 PP, 1996 BBYA
Levels: BL 7–12, SLJ 6–9

Annotation: A Welsh boy, whose tongue had been cut out, is sold into slavery by his uncle. He learns to read and write, and becomes a scribe and the "adopted" son to Earl Harold, the future King of England.

Booktalk: The anger inside of Evyn had yet to abate. He still thought of himself as a free man, trained to tell the tales of the Welsh people. Evyn tried not to think of how his uncle's drunken outburst had destroyed his world. The Britons had mistaken his father for Uncle Morgan and had killed him. They then turned their knives on Evyn and cut his tongue out. Before they could kidnap him, Uncle Morgan had rescued Evyn, only to sell him for a bag of coins. Earl Harold's Lady treated him kindly, but he could not accept that he was a slave. He did not want to be "a silent shadow," as the monk called him. Little did Evyn know whose "silent shadow" he would become.

Curriculum Connection: History

Evyn is with King Harold at the Battle of Hastings. Have students do research on King Harold and this battle to determine what role a scribe, such as Evyn, would have had. Would he have been found next to the king had he not been his adopted son?

Anderson, Laurie Halse, *Fever 1793.*

Simon & Schuster, 2000, 256pp. $16. ISBN: 0-689-83858-1. Aladdin, 2002, 256pp. $5.99. ISBN: 0-689-84891-9
Subjects: Epidemics, Grandparents, Mothers and Daughters, Race Relations
Genre: Historical
List: 2001 BBYA
Levels: BL 7–12, SLJ 6–10, VOYA 7–12

Annotation: Fifteen-year-old Mattie survives the 1793 yellow fever epidemic in Philadelphia, but loses her grandfather and does not know where her mother is. With the help of their African-American cook, Mattie is determined to make the family coffeehouse a success.

Booktalk: After her mother is stricken with yellow fever, Mattie's grandfather accompanies her to a farm in the country. On the way, they are stopped by armed men who will not allow wagons carrying yellow fever victims through their town. Discovering that her grandfather is running a fever, the wagon driver dumps them out on the side of the road so he and his wife can escape the epidemic that is killing Philadelphia residents by the thousands. Mattie is devastated when she discovers that the food and water the cook had packed for them is still in the wagon. Grandfather is delirious and running a high fever, and Mattie is starving. Using the skills her grandfather taught her, Mattie is able to find water and berries, but this is not going to be enough to keep them alive.

Curriculum Connections: Health, History

Have students research the yellow fever epidemic of 1793 in relation to the misconceptions people, including physicians, had during that period, about yellow fever. How would an outbreak of yellow fever be handled in modern-day Philadelphia?

4 Anderson, Laurie Halse, *Speak.*

Farrar, Straus & Giroux, 1999, 198pp. $16. ISBN: 0-374-37152-0. Penguin Putnam, 2001, 208pp. $7.99. ISBN: 0-14-131088-X

Subjects: Emotional Problems, High Schools, Rape
Genre: Realistic
Lists: 2000 BBYA, 2000 QP
Award: Michael L. Printz Honor
Levels: BL 8–12, SLJ 8 & Up

Annotation: Melinda was too traumatized to admit to the police that she had been raped the night she called 911. Because she didn't tell them or anyone else why she reported the party, the other students ostracize or torment her, making her first year of high school miserable. When the rapist tries to attack her again, she finally speaks out.

Booktalk: Freshman year of high school isn't easy for anyone, but for Melinda Sordino it was especially hard. During the first football pep rally she attended, Melinda turned around when she heard someone harshly asking her if she was Melinda Sordino. Melinda slowly nodded her head. She knew there was more coming from this girl with the black fingernails who was smacking gum in her face. The girl poked Melinda—hard—and loudly asked her if she was the one who had called the cops at the end of the year summer party. There was no point in answering—everyone in the bleachers had turned to look at Melinda. They all knew she had placed the call. Her throat started to close up and she could not speak, just like the night she called 911.

Curriculum Connection: English

Have students look up the definition of "unspeakable" in several different dictionaries and then write an essay discussing whether they think *Speak* is an appropriate title for this novel. Does the title "define" what the story is about?

5 Atkins, Catherine, *When Jeff Comes Home.*

G.P. Putnam, 1999, 231pp. $17.99. ISBN: 0-399-23366-0

Subjects: Child Sexual Abuse, Fathers and Sons, Kidnapping, Self-esteem
Genre: Realistic
List: 2000 BBYA
Levels: BL 10–12, SLJ 10 & Up

Annotation: Almost three years after he had been abducted and sexually abused, 16-year-old Jeff is returned home. He does not admit he has been abused until his kidnapper is caught and testifies that Jeff was a willing partner.

Booktalk: Ray followed him down the road, with his headlights off, as Jeff walked through the rain, back to the house he had grown up in, back to a family he had not seen in almost three years. Ray's world was all he had known. Jeff walked into the yard, but he couldn't walk up the front steps. What was he supposed to say? Ray tapped his horn, and Jeff automatically plastered on a smile and walked back to the car. But Ray didn't want him back; he wanted him to go in. Jeff walked to the porch and watched Ray's car pull out of sight. That's when the door flew open and a man shouted at him to put his hands up. Jeff just stood there with his head down until his father recognized him and pulled him into a hug. This is what Jeff had dreamed of the whole time he had been gone, but now he felt nothing, except cold and ashamed.

Atwater-Rhodes, Amelia, *In the Forests of the Night.* — 6

Delacorte, 1999, 147pp. $8.95. ISBN: 0-385-32674-2. Bantam Doubleday Dell, 2000, 160pp. $4.99. ISBN: 0-440-22816-6

Subjects: Brothers and Sisters, Time Travel, Vampires
Genres: Horror, Supernatural
List: 2000 QP
Levels: BL 7–12, SLJ 8 & Up, VOYA 6–9

Annotation: Shape-shifting teenage vampire, Risika, time travels between present day Massachusetts and 1684, when she died and was turned into a vampire. She is seeking revenge against Aubrey, the vampire she feels is responsible for the murder of her twin brother.

Booktalk: Risika laughed over the human myths about vampires as she crawled into her bed. She didn't sleep in a coffin and she didn't worry about burning up in the sunlight. Garlic was obnoxious smelling because her sense of smell was 20 times better than a bloodhound's, but she certainly wasn't afraid of it. Risika wore a silver ring on her finger, and she had attended Christian services in a church. She would give the humans one of their myths—if someone actually hammered a stake into her heart, she probably would die. But then again, she didn't play with humans, or stakes for that matter.

Curriculum Connection: English

Atwater-Rhodes was 14 when she wrote In the *Forests of the Night.* She is not the only teenage author of books that appeal to teens. Have students research other young authors, such as S. E. Hinton, or the writing and reading preferences of favorite authors when they were teenagers.

7 Bauer, Joan, *Rules of the Road.*

Putnam, 1998, 201pp. $15.99. ISBN: 0-399-23140-4. Puffin, 2000, 208pp. $4.99. ISBN: 0-698-11828-6
Subjects: Alcoholism, Automobile Driving, The Elderly
Genres: Humor, Realistic
Lists: 2000 B of BBYA, 1999 BBYA, 1999 QP
Levels: BL 6–10, SLJ 7 & Up, VOYA 10–12

Annotation: Sixteen-year-old Jenna learns more than how to handle a Cadillac the summer she drives an elderly owner of a chain of shoe stores from Chicago to Dallas. Jenna learns she also can handle dealing with her alcoholic father.

Booktalk: My dad has never been there for me. When he does come around, he is drunk and embarrasses me. I thought I would die the day he showed up at the Chicago shoe store where I work. He was loud and obnoxious, and all I could think of was getting him out of there before Mrs. Gladstone, the owner of the store, heard him. I was sure I was going to get fired when I saw the disgusted look on her face as she came out of the back room to see what all the commotion was about. But that isn't what happened. Instead, Mrs. Gladstone hired me to drive her to Dallas, Texas. I don't know how well this is going to work—I'm not even sure I can back that huge Cadillac out of her garage!

8 Bauer, Joan, *Thwonk.*

Bantam Doubleday Dell, 1996, 215pp. $3.99. ISBN: 0-440-21980-9
Subjects: High Schools, Photography, Relationships
Genres: Humor, Romance
Lists: 1999 PP, 1996 BBYA
Levels: BL 7–10, SLJ 7–10

Annotation: When Cupid appears and offers academic, artistic, or romantic assistance to photographer A. J., she makes the wrong choice. When Cupid shoots Peter, the boy A. J. is crazy about, with one of his arrows, A. J. discovers that having someone infatuated with her isn't as wonderful as she thought it would be.

Booktalk: I should have listened to Jonathan when he told me that love isn't all it's drummed up to be, but no, I had to insist he shoot Peter with one of his arrows so he would invite me to the King of Hearts Dance. By the time Valentine's Day arrived, I was sick of Peter. When he showed up where I work, it was all I could do to keep my breakfast down. He walked in and dreamily called my name. I responded with, "Yo," hoping he would go away, but no such luck. He had a bouquet of white roses as big as a car! I took off running for the kitchen, with him hot on my trail, holding out a box of chocolates. I knew I had to take aggressive action—before he could start singing, I jammed a biscotti in his mouth. I had absolutely had it with him shrieking his love for me. If you had told me, before I asked Jonathan to shoot Peter with his cupid's arrow, that I would ever say I was loved too much by Peter, I would have said you were crazy. But there really is such a thing as too much of a good thing!

Curriculum Connection: English

A. J. got exactly what she wished for—for the guy she was infatuated with to fall in love with her. Have students write about an experience when they finally got something they were wanting and wishing for, only to find out it was not at all what they expected.

Bennett, Cherie, *Life in the Fat Lane.*

Delacorte, 1998, 260pp. $15.95. ISBN: 0-385-32274-7. Bantam Doubleday Dell, 1999, 272pp. $4.99. ISBN: 0-440-22029-7
Subjects: Eating Disorders, Family Problems, High Schools, Moving, Weight Control
Genre: Realistic
List: 1999 BBYA
Levels: BL 6–9, SLJ 8 & Up, VOYA 7–12

9

Annotation: Sixteen-year-old Lara, winner of beauty pageants, begins to gain weight uncontrollably because of a metabolic disorder. No matter how little she eats or how much she exercises, she keeps gaining weight. Then her parents move to Detroit and she discovers firsthand how fat girls in school are treated.

Booktalk: Lara has no clue what is happening to her. One day she is the perfect girl at school—a perfect size six, with a perfect boyfriend, and a perfectly good chance at being the Homecoming Queen. Then she begins to gain weight. She thinks it is her allergy medication, but when she stops taking it, not only does she *not* lose weight, she gains even more. Friends at school are beginning to look at her funny, and she is wondering if her boyfriend, Jett, even wants to be with her. And now her parents have decided to move, and she is going to be the new girl in school, the new FAT girl in school. Life has certainly changed for Lara—she is experiencing life in the fat lane.

Curriculum Connection: Health

Lara has a metabolic disorder that causes weight gain. Have students research other unusual metabolic disorders or rare diseases and how the victims suffer. For example, how does lack of knowledge by other people make having the disease or disorder even more difficult?

10 Block, Francesca Lia, *Baby Be-Bop.*

HarperCollins, 1995, 106pp. $13.89. ISBN: 0-0-06-024880-7. HarperTrophy, 1997, 112pp. $4.95. ISBN: 0-06-447176-4
Subjects: Ghosts, Grandparents, Homosexuality
Genres: Realistic, Supernatural
List: 1996 BBYA
Levels: BL 8–12, SLJ 10 & Up

Annotation: Sixteen-year-old Dirk falls in love with his best friend, Pup, but is shunned by him. So he cuts his hair into a Mohawk and starts wearing leather and chains. Eventually he learns to accept his homosexuality through the love of his grandmother and the stories the ghosts of his ancestors tell him.

Booktalk: Fear is tangible. You can even taste it. Dirk knew fear—the fear of being different. He knew how important it was to be picked first. He knew that the weak and skinny guys got picked last for teams. Sometimes they even went home with black eyes and bloody noses. So Dirk knew the best thing he could do was keep to himself so that they would never notice him and he would never have to show he was afraid. Then he met Pup and they roamed the streets of Los Angeles together. They got brown from the sun, and lean and strong. They rode skateboards, wore torn jeans, and were dreamed about by the popular girls. But Dirk still knew fear—fear that Pup would leave when he found out the truth.

11 Block, Francesca Lia, *I Was a Teenage Fairy.*

HarperCollins, 1998, 186pp. $14.89. ISBN: 0-06-027748-3. HarperTrophy, 2000, 192pp. $7.95. ISBN: 0-06-440862-0
Subjects: Child Sexual Abuse, Fairies, Mothers and Daughters
Genres: Fantasy, Realistic
List: 1999 QP
Levels: BL 8–12, SLJ 9 & Up

Annotation: Sixteen-year-old Barbie has a pinkie size fairy, Mab, who helps her deal with her domineering mother and the memories of the photographer who sexually molested her when she was 11. Mab departs when Barbie falls in love with Todd and begins her live anew.

Booktalk: Mab didn't know much about the human world. As a fairy, she was a diva in the world of ladybugs and butterflies. She hadn't learned a whole lot about the Big World, but she did know it was a much uglier place than she wanted to believe, especially when her human, Barbie, held up the picture of Hamilton Waverly. He was one of those things that should have stayed under a rock. His type of human had no respect for the smallest and most delicate members of the race. Mab helped Barbie touch the lighted match to the picture and watch it burn.

Block, Francesca Lia, *Violet & Claire.* |12|

HarperCollins, 1999, 169pp. $14.89. ISBN: 0-06-027750-5. HarperTrophy, 2000, 176pp. $6.95. ISBN: 0-06-447253-1
Subjects: Authorship, Friendship
Genre: Realistic
List: 2000 QP
Levels: BL 10 & Up, SLJ 9 & Up

Annotation: Seventeen-year-old Violet and her friend Claire get caught up in the fast lane in Los Angeles, severing their friendship. Violet becomes a scriptwriter and Claire falls in love with her poetry teacher. The story is told through shifting perspectives and concludes with the girls finding each other again.

Booktalk: The laptop went with her everywhere. Violet was sitting at school working on her screenplay when she saw her. A tiny girl wearing a Tinkerbell T-shirt, with her blonde hair on top of her head in a goofy ponytail. That's when Violet decided that Claire would be the star in her movie. It wasn't until she rescued her future leading lady from a group of harassing students that Violet noticed the iridescent gauze and wire fairy wings on Claire's back. Talk about opposites attracting!

Blume, Judy, *Forever.* |13|

Simon & Schuster, 1982, 216pp. $16. ISBN: 0-02-711030-3. Pocket, 1989, 220pp. $4.50. ISBN: 0-671-69530-4
Subject: Sexual Relationships
Genres: Realistic, Romance
List: 1994 B of BBYA
Levels: No current interest levels available

Annotation: Seventeen-year-olds Katherine and Michael fall in love and they begin a sexual relationship. Katherine goes away to summer camp, becomes attracted to another boy, and discovers that first loves aren't always forever.

Booktalk: How does a girl resist a guy who tells her that she is delicious after their first kiss? Well, Katherine cannot resist Michael and thus begins their relationship and exploration into sex. Katherine is sure she wants to spend the rest of her life with Michael, but she begins to question this idea when she goes away for the summer and becomes attracted to another guy. She begins to ask herself, "How do you know when love really is forever?"

Curriculum Connection: Health

Judy Blume wrote this book in 1975 for her daughter, who was 14. At the time this book was written, pregnancy was the major concern of sexual activity. Pregnancy is certainly still an issue, but what concerns are present today that are not addressed in this still-popular book written over 25 years ago?

14 Brooks, Terry, *Magic Kingdom for Sale: Sold!*

(Magic Kingdom of Landover Series, #1) Ballantine, 1987, 373pp. $6.99. ISBN: 0-345-31758-0
Subjects: Death, Dragons, Fairies, Kings, Magic, Self-esteem
Genre: Fantasy
Booklist: 2000 B of BBYA
Level: Adult

Annotation: Ben, a disgruntled lawyer who is grieving over the death of his wife and unborn child, buys a magic kingdom from a Christmas catalog. He discovers it is in ruin and inhabited by a diverse group of species in need of a leader to defeat the Iron Mark and unite the kingdom.

Booktalk: Ben couldn't believe it. He paid one million dollars for a magic kingdom out of a Christmas Wish Book so he could escape the problems of the real world, only to discover he is now king of a land in ruin. His Court Magician is incompetent, his Court Scribe is a talking dog, the different groups in the kingdom are fighting, and the beautiful woman he thinks he may be falling in love with turns into a tree. On top of all that, there is no money-back guarantee on this supposedly magic kingdom.

Curriculum Connection: Science

When Ben enters the Magic Kingdom, he discovers it in ruin. The different groups of people are feuding, with many of their concerns relating to the environment. Have students compare the concerns of the residents of the Magic Kingdom with the concerns we have today about Earth's ecological systems.

Burgess, Melvin, *Smack.*

Holt, 1998, 326pp. $16.95. ISBN: 0-8050-5801-X. Morrow/Avon, 1999, 304pp. $6.99. ISBN: 0-380-73223-8
Subjects: Drug Abuse, Pregnancy
Genre: Realistic
List: 2002 PP, 1999 BBYA
Level: SLJ 10 & Up

Annotation: Two teenage runaways, 14-year-olds Tar and Gemma, move in with a group of squatters in Bristol, England, and become addicted to heroin. The story of their four years of heroin addiction is told through multiple voices. Carnegie Medal winner under the title *Junk*.

Booktalk: My parents haven't got a clue. They think just because I spent the night with Tar that I had sex with him. I spent the night with him because his father had beat him up again and he was running away. If I had wanted to have sex with Tar, I certainly wouldn't do it when we were saying goodbye. I know he's in love with me, but I don't think I love him. Anyway, all hell broke loose when I got home the next day. Dad is still raging about how a girl's reputation is her greatest asset. Maybe I should rethink my decision to run away with Tar. It would be more fun than dealing with my parents on a daily basis.

Cadnum, Michael, *Rundown.*

Viking, 1999, 168pp. $15.99. ISBN: 0-670-88377-8. Penguin Putnam, 2001, 176pp. $5.99. ISBN: 0-14-131087-1
Subjects: Parent and Child, Rape, Self-esteem, Sisters, Track and Field
Genres: Realistic, Sports
List: 2000 QP
Levels: BL 9–12, SLJ 10 & Up

Annotation: To get the attention of her highly successful parents as they prepare for her older sister's wedding, 16-year-old Jennifer fakes an attempted attack by a serial rapist while she is out running, but the female police officer knows she is lying.

Booktalk: From the outside looking in, Jennifer Thayer has the perfect family. Her mother is a successful businesswoman, her father is a chef with a syndicated TV show, and her older sister is marrying Mr. Perfect. So why is Jennifer standing in the bushes on the Berkeley campus of the University of California, waiting for the opportune moment to throw herself into the thicket and roll down the hill to get scratched and bruised? Let's just see big sister try to outshine Jennifer's limelight as the courageous teenage runner who successfully fought off a serial rapist. What Jennifer doesn't know yet, as she rolls down that hill, is she soon will be running from a real pursuer.

17 Carter, Alden R., *Between a Rock and a Hard Place.*

Scholastic, 1995, 213pp. $14.95. ISBN: 0-590-48684-5. Scholastic, 1999, 224pp. $4.99. ISBN: 0-590-37486-9
Subjects: Camping, Diabetes, Fathers and Sons, Survival
Genre: Adventure
List: 1996 BBYA
Levels: BL 6–9, SLJ 7 & Up

Annotation: Fifteen-year-old cousins Mark and Randy go on a canoeing trip in the Boundary Waters in Northern Minnesota and lose their gear, including Randy's insulin. Mark has to get them back to civilization before Randy goes into insulin shock.

Booktalk: The fact that Randy's father made his cousin Mark leader of this stupid expedition was really irritating. It wasn't like he wanted to go on this canoe trip their fathers insisted was a family tradition. To top it off, they were being laughed at before they even got out of eyesight. Randy's dad was bent over holding his sides he was laughing so hard as these two city boys tried to keep their canoe straight in the wind. Will these two city boys survive the northern wilderness or will a bear, bad weather, and the loss of their gear end this trip in tragedy?

Curriculum Connection: Health

Randy is a diabetic and during the boys' canoe trip they lose his insulin. Have students do research on what happens when a person goes into insulin shock and how, if they were Mark, they could have helped Randy deal with the side effects until they could get to safety. Along with diabetes, have students research other diseases teens suffer from, and how to deal with them in emergency situations.

18 Carter, Alden R., *Up Country.*

Scholastic 1998, 256pp. $4.99. ISBN: 0-590-43638-4
Subjects: Alcoholism, Family Problems, Mothers and Sons
Genre: Realistic
List: B of BBYA
Level: BL 8–12

Annotation: Sixteen-year-old Carl's mother is arrested and put in an alcoholism detox center. He is sent to a small town in northern Wisconsin, far away from his Milwaukee home and the stolen electronics he had been repairing in the basement.

Booktalk: Carl panicked when he saw the cop's blue uniform through the basement window. He quickly looked to make sure the broken dashboard pieces from the car stereos were not in view. The cop kept knocking at the door, but his mom didn't answer it. Maybe this time something really did happen to her rather than her coming home in the middle of the night, drunk. Carl went upstairs and answered the door. The cop said that his mother had gotten into a fight the night before and laid open a guy's head with a beer bottle. She ran out the back door and when the cops caught up with her, she kicked one of them in the crotch before she gave herself up. She was going into a detox center and Carl into a foster home if he didn't have any family. Before he knew it, Carl was on a bus headed for Hicksville, in northern Wisconsin, to live with relatives—relatives he knew nothing about.

Cascone, A. G., *If He Hollers.*

Morrow/Avon, 1995, 182pp. $3.99. ISBN: 0-380-77753-3
Subjects: Death, Kidnapping, Mental Illness
Genres: Horror, Mystery
List: 1997 YAC
Levels: No current interest levels available

19

Annotation: Ten years after being kidnapped at a neighborhood birthday party, 17-year-old Bobby is back to kill the partygoers one at a time, all except for the girl who screamed when she saw the kidnapper take him.

Booktalk: He is watching them from the woods. It's Stacey Patterson's seventeenth birthday party, but the scene doesn't look a whole lot different from her seventh birthday party. They didn't know they were being watched back then, and they don't know they are being watched now. He is looking forward to killing each of them, one by one, all except for Mel. He has a special place in his heart for Mel, so it will be different when he catches her. He is going to keep her forever and ever and make her love him, just like he has loved her, forever and ever.

20 Chbosky, Stephen, *The Perks of Being a Wallflower.*

MTV/Pocket, 1999, 213pp. $12. ISBN: 0-671-02734-4
Subjects: Child Sexual Abuse, Emotional Problems, High Schools, Letter Writing, Self-esteem
Genre: Realistic
Lists: 2002 PP, 2000 BBYA, 2000 QP
Level: SLJ 9 & Up

Annotation: Charlie, a gifted but troubled teen, chronicles his freshman year in high school via letters to an unknown recipient, as he watches, more than interacts, with his family, his therapist, his English teacher, and a close-knit group of friends.

Booktalk: Charlie finds it easier to sit back at a party and watch—watch how Patrick and Sam and the rest of his friends are feeling, and play music to match their moods. Charlie moves through life watching until he is forced to act when others are in need. Charlie is the one who takes his older sister to the abortion clinic when her boyfriend says he wants nothing to do with her. Charlie is the one who jumps into the fray when his gay friend, Patrick, is being beat up in the cafeteria by the football players. But for Charlie, it is a reaction, not an action, that triggers the childhood memories, the ones Charlie has had buried for so many years.

Curriculum Connections: English, Psychology

Charlie writes letters to express his feelings about life, but they are never answered. Have students choose one of Charlie's letters and respond to it, suggesting how he can adjust to the changes that are occurring in his life.

21 Cochran, Thomas, *Roughnecks.*

Harcourt Brace, 1997, 256pp. $15. ISBN: 0-15-201433-0. Harcourt Brace, 1999, 248pp. $6. ISBN: 0-15-202200-7
Subjects: Football, Relationships, Self-esteem
Genre: Sports
List: 1999 YAC
Levels: BL 8–12, SLJ 6–9, VOYA 6–12

Annotation: Travis Cody is facing the final game of his high school football career, his last chance to redeem himself for a play that cost his team, the Louisiana Oil Camp Roughnecks, an undefeated season the prior year, and he is afraid he won't succeed.

Booktalk: Someone has been calling Travis Cody on the phone, haunting his waking and sleeping hours. The caller tells him that he blew it, that he choked when his team needed him. Travis doesn't need anyone telling him that his bad play cost the Oil Camp Roughnecks an undefeated season last year. He is well aware of his failures. It doesn't matter that he is in excruciating back pain. He has to prove his worth as a football player, both to the town and to himself. The last game of his senior year is almost here, and it is time for Travis to face down his nemesis from last year—Jericho Grooms. What if he chokes again?

Conford, Ellen, *Crush.*

22

HarperCollins, 1998, 138pp. $14.95. ISBN: 0-06-025414-9. HarperCollins, 1999, 144pp. $4.95. ISBN: 0-06-440778-0
Subjects: High Schools, Relationships
Genres: Humor, Romance
Lists: 1999 QP, 2000 PP
Levels: BL 7–12, SLJ 5–8

Annotation: The chapters of this novel are divided up into nine romantic, and sometimes humorous, episodes in the lives of Cutter's Forge High School students as they prepare for the Valentine's Day Sweetheart Stomp.

Booktalk: Have you ever wondered where the money goes when you buy raffle tickets? Will never thought about it until after his girlfriend's father tersely told him not to give her any money. He thought that was a strange thing for Linda's dad to say, but it wasn't until Linda brought him the write-up on Little Billy Thigpen from Boise, Montana, that he got really suspicious. Billy was supposedly a kid with a mysterious disease that prevented him from metabolizing fat, and his family needed money to help buy the fatty foods to keep him alive. After seeing the write-up, Will was sure his gorgeous girlfriend was a scam artist. Linda should have checked a map; Boise is in Idaho, not Montana. She also didn't know Will and his friend Matt were going to scare her right out of her newest moneymaking scheme.

Curriculum Connections: English, Psychology
   Read aloud the chapter "The Gifts of the Mangy" to the students and then have them read O. Henry's short story "The Gift of the Magi." Compare and contrast the story line and gifts given in relation to the different eras in which the stories are set.

23 Cook, Karin, *What Girls Learn.*

Random House, 1998, 304pp. $13. ISBN: 0-6797-6944-7
Subjects: Cancer, Death, Mothers and Daughters, Sisters, Stepfamilies
Genre: Historical
Lists: 1998 Alex, 1998 BBYA
Level: Adult

Annotation: Twelve-year-old Tilden narrates the story of two sisters dealing with a new stepfather, their move to New York from Atlanta, and the slow death of their mother from breast cancer, which was not openly discussed in the 1960s.

Booktalk: Tilden didn't know what to make of Nick when he drove up in a limousine and stepped out from behind the tinted windows with his dark wavy hair and sunglasses. She couldn't believe he was actually expecting her and Elizabeth to accept him as their new father. Tilden's world was turned upside down with her mother's decision to move in with Nick, leaving behind their sultry Atlanta home for the snowy streets of Long Island. But when her mother's tests came back positive, her world really began to spin out of control.

Curriculum Connections: Health, Psychology

The subject of breast cancer is not hushed up today as it was in the 1960s and 1970s, nor do as many people die of this type of cancer today. Have students research the advances that have taken place in relation to breast cancer treatment, including the psychological impact of a diagnosis of breast cancer for a woman.

24 Cooney, Caroline B., *Both Sides of Time.*

Delacorte, 1995, 210pp. $10.95. ISBN: 0-385-32174-0. Bantam Doubleday Dell, 1997, 224pp. $4.99. ISBN: 0-440-21932-9
Subjects: Relationships, Time Travel
Genres: Historical, Romance, Supernatural
List: 1999 PP
Level: BL 6–10

Annotation: Annie is tired of her car-crazy boyfriend, who ignores her. She wants to live in a more romantic time. But when she finds herself time traveling back into the 1880s, she discovers there are consequences to being romantically involved in two centuries. Companion novel to *Out of Time* (Bantam, 1997).

Booktalk: Annie had been reading every advice column she could find. She knew two things she wasn't supposed to do. One was to try to change other people. The other was to mind your own business. But Annie wasn't about to do either. She was tired of being the only romantic one in this relationship. There was Sean—dressed in a white T-shirt and jeans, surrounded by old cars, and he hadn't even noticed she had arrived. Oh, how she would love to see him in a starched white collar, gold cuff links, and black tails. After all, they were standing on the grounds of an old mansion. But why was she even bothering to think that way? She was a romantic in the wrong century. Annie was about to find out what things were like a hundred years ago when this very mansion's floors shone, and the ballroom was lit up and filled with music. One second Annie was envisioning Sean in a tux, and the next second she had blacked out and fallen into the year 1895 and right into the arms of another man. She would soon discover that there are consequences for falling in love in two different centuries.

Curriculum Connection: History

Fantasy novels often include time travel to an earlier time. Have students choose a historically based time travel novel, such as *Both Sides of Time* (Delacorte, 1995), *Out of Time* (Bantam, 1997), or *Mr. Was* (Simon & Schuster, 1996). Have them look for incidents that occurred while the time traveler was there that made it evident the character could not have been from that time period.

Cooney, Caroline B., *Driver's Ed.*

25

Delacorte, 1994, 184pp. $15.95. ISBN: 0-385-32087-6. Dell, 1996, 208pp. $5.50. ISBN: 0-440-21981-7
Subjects: Accidents, Automobile Driving, Death, High Schools
Genre: Realistic
List: Author's Choice
Levels: BL 7–12, SLJ 7 & Up

Annotation: After two driver's education students help steal a stop sign, a young mother is killed at the intersection. At first the students try hiding their guilt, but eventually they come forward, admitting they committed the crime and taking responsibility for the consequences.

Booktalk: Morgan and Remy knew Nickie was a gutter rat, and after tonight they would never spend another minute with him. But right now they were going to enjoy the thrill of stealing signs. They already had Morgan's sign that said THICKLY SETTLED. When Nickie asked Remy what sign she wanted, she shyly said MORGAN LANE. At first Remy tried to pry the street sign loose, but the bolts wouldn't turn. So she got down and held Morgan's ankles as he stood on the roof of Nickie's car to get the sign down. Then it was Nickie's turn to pick a sign he wanted. Nickie chose a STOP sign from Cherry Road. Remy hadn't even known this narrow and almost invisible road intersected busy Warren Road. Remy and Morgan went to sleep that night dreaming about the pleasure and thrill of their first kiss, which they also stole that night. But they were soon to be experiencing a nightmare caused by their after-dark escapade.

Curriculum Connection: Psychology

Remy and Morgan eventually admit to having been involved in stealing the stop sign that resulted in the death of a young mother. They visit her husband and find a grieving man who wants them to be as miserable as he is and to remember what they did for the rest of their lives. Have students discuss their reactions to a similar situation, including facing the anger of the grieving husband.

26 Cooney, Caroline B., *The Terrorist.*

Scholastic, 1997, 198pp. $15.95. ISBN: 0-590-22853-6. Scholastic, 1999, 198pp. $4.50. ISBN: 0-590-22854-4
Subjects: Brothers and Sisters, High Schools, Murder, Terrorism
Genres: Mystery, Realistic
List: 1998 QP
Levels: BL 6–10, SLJ 5–10

Annotation: Sixteen-year-old Laura, an American student at an International School in London, is determined to find out who was responsible for the terrorist bomb that killed her little brother. She begins to suspect the other students in her high school, but does not realize the killer is a female student she is helping escape to the United States.

Booktalk: No one saw who handed the package wrapped in brown paper to her brother. Billy died when the bomb went off, but life went on around his tragic death. Commuters continued to leave London's Underground, and the killer easily slipped away. Laura couldn't deal with the idea that someone had targeted her brother to die. One minute she was crying, and the next she was so angry her whole body shook. She wanted revenge; she burned with it. Laura was going to find the killer, and he was going to die just the way Billy did. But her anger turned to fear when the police officer quietly but sternly told her to step away from the window. They still didn't know if her family, not just Billy, was the target.

Curriculum Connections: Government, History

Laura is a typical American teenager until her brother dies. Then she begins to look around the International School she attends in London and realizes that students from certain countries have nothing to do with each other, due to politics and religion. Have the students create a cafeteria floor plan for Laura's school with students from various countries from the Middle East, Europe, and other parts of the world and where they would probably sit. Have students discuss which students from various countries would not be sitting together.

Cooney, Caroline B., *The Voice on the Radio.*

Delacorte, 1996, 183pp. $15.95. ISBN: 0-385-32213-5. Bantam Doubleday Dell, 1998, 192pp. $5.50. ISBN: 0-440-21977-9

Subjects: Brothers and Sisters, Friendship, Kidnapping, Parent and Child
Genre: Realistic
Lists: 1998 YAC, 1997 BBYA
Levels: BL 7–10, SLJ 6–10

Annotation: Sixteen-year-old Janie's boyfriend, Reeve, wants to be a radio DJ so badly that he betrays her trust by talking about her childhood kidnapping on his college radio show. Janie hears his show and confronts him. With the help of her parents Janie comes to terms with what he did. Companion novel to *The Face on the Milk Carton* (Laurel Leaf, 1991) and *Whatever Happened to Janie?* (Delacorte, 1993).

Booktalk: Reeve went blank—he couldn't think of a single thing to say and he still had 46 minutes of airtime to fill. Then he started talking about his girlfriend, Janie, and how she found out she had been kidnapped when she was three years old. He had his college listening audience spellbound. He was told he had a great radio voice. There were 39 callers asking for more about Janie. And this was just his first night. The airwaves were his. Then he thought about Janie and what she would think of his broadcast. She was such a private person that even the counselors couldn't get her to talk about what happened to her. For a moment he felt like he was drowning, but he quickly convinced himself that she would never hear his college radio station "Janie" broadcasts.

Curriculum Connections: Government, Psychology

Reeve broke Janie's confidence by talking about her childhood kidnapping. He made her private agony public on the radio. Have students compare what Reeve did to recent events in the national news. Does ethical behavior in relation to a person's private life exist in the United States?

28 Cormier, Robert, *Heroes.*

Delacorte, 1998, 135pp. $15.95. ISBN: 0-385-32590-8. Dell, 2000, 144pp. $5.50. ISBN: 0-440-22769-0
Subjects: Physically Handicapped, Rape, Suicide, War, World War II
Genre: Historical
Lists: 1999 BBYA, 1999 QP
Levels: BL 7–12, SLJ 9 & Up, VOYA 7–12

Annotation: Eighteen-year-old Francis returns home from World War II with severe facial injuries from falling on a grenade in France. Now a bitter war hero, he has come home to kill the man who raped his girlfriend years before. But when he has the chance, he realizes it isn't worth it. The man who was once his hero commits suicide.

Booktalk: My name is Francis and I just returned from fighting the war in France. Everyone thinks I am a hero because I threw myself on a grenade and saved the lives of many soldiers. I don't deserve the Silver Star for heroism because I knew exactly what I was doing when I threw myself on that grenade—I was trying to commit suicide. I couldn't even do that right. So here I am back home with half a face. My eyes are fine, so I can see, and I can hear because I have eardrums, but as far as ears go I just have bits of dangling flesh. The lack of ears doesn't bother me as much as not having a nose. I have these two small caves in the middle of my face, and they run a lot so I wear a bandage around that part of my face. My teeth are gone, and the dentures they gave me don't fit because my gums keep shrinking. But really none of this matters because I have come home to seek revenge. That's all that really matters.

Curriculum Connection: History
   Francis returned from the war a bitter man, but he was only 15 when he enlisted in the U. S. Army. Have students research the numbers of, and stories about, young soldiers in the Revolutionary and Civil Wars as well as World Wars I and II. Why would a teenage boy want to enlist in the military?

29 Cormier, Robert, *In the Middle of the Night.*

Bantam Doubleday Dell, 1997, 182pp. $4.99. ISBN: 0-440-22686-4
Subjects: Accidents, Mental Illness, Physically Handicapped
Genre: Mystery, Realistic
Lists: 1996 BBYA, 1996 QP
Levels: BL 10–12, SLJ 7 & Up

Annotation: Sixteen-year-old Denny answers the phone and is seduced by the soft sounds of Lulu's voice until she convinces him to meet her, the deranged survivor of a theater fire she blames on Denny's father. Denny is trapped with the woman, but her brother stops her from killing him. Both the brother and sister then die in a fire.

Booktalk: He wondered what she said to the man during those middle-of-the-night phone calls and why he listened to her. Every year she called him around Halloween. He hoped that maybe this year would be different. But when he heard her tell him that the sins of the father would be visited upon the son, he knew her revenge was far from over. Even when he tried to convince her not to torment the man's teenage son, Lulu told him that she had been the one who died, not him. Sooner or later he knew Denny, the man's son, would pick up that phone and be sucked into his sister's insane world.

Cross, Gillian, *Tightrope.*

Holiday, 1999, 216pp. $16.95. ISBN: 0-8234-1512-0. HarperCollins, 2001, 304pp. $5.95. ISBN: 0-0644-7272-8
Subjects: Family Problems, Gangs, Mothers and Daughters
Genres: Mystery, Realistic
List: 2002 PP, 2001 BBYA
Levels: BL 7–12, SLJ 7–10

Annotation: Fourteen-year-old Ashley is taking care of her ill mother, but sneaks out at night to paint her "tag" on the walls of her urban British neighborhood. When she discovers someone is stalking her, she goes to the local gang leader for help. But her involvement with the gang results in even more trouble; the gang leader is involved in the stalking.

Booktalk: Ashley knew her mother might hear her sneaking out late at night, but the thrill of what she did was too strong for her to stop. She put the spray cans in her backpack and slipped out the back door. She snuck through the dark streets until she found the building she was looking for, and started to climb. She knew if she made one false step she would be splattered on the sidewalk below. But she was willing to walk this tightrope for the high she would get tomorrow when the neighborhood saw the tag she had painted on the wall—CINDY—in big, bright orange, red, and yellow letters.

Curriculum Connection: Sociology

Tightrope is set in an urban area of England. Ashley walks to school through a neighborhood where drugs and violence are a problem. There is a gang in the area with a leader who controls what happens in the neighborhood. Obviously gangs are not only a problem in the United States. Have students research gang activity in other countries of the world and how foreign gangs' styles of clothes, initiation rites, and membership is similar to or different from the gangs in the United States.

31. Crutcher, Chris, *Ironman*.

HarperCollins, 1995, 192pp. $15. ISBN: 0-688-13503-X. Bantam Doubleday Dell, 1996, 228pp. $4.50. ISBN: 0-440-21971-X

Subjects: Fathers and Sons, Football, Friendship, High Schools, Letter Writing
Genres: Realistic, Sports
Lists: 2000 B of BBYA, 1999 PP, 1996 BBYA, 1996 QP
Levels: BL 8–12, SLJ 9 & Up

Annotation: Seventeen-year-old Bo Brewster's battle with his domineering father has gone on for so long that his anger is leaking out onto the football field and into the classroom. Bo is required to attend an anger management class, where he discovers true friends and learns to come to terms with his anger.

Booktalk: When Bo is told that his anger comes from his own life and that is he going to deal with it in anger management classes, Bo wakes up from a nightmare that started with a slamming door—a slammed door that sent his napping father into a rage. He demanded that the then nine-year-old Bo close the door quietly 10 times in a row. Bo made it through nine, but the tenth time he slammed it so hard it cracked three windows. The isolation then began. Bo was to attend school, but otherwise he was to stay in his room. He was not even allowed to speak to his sister. For almost seven months Bo didn't exist to his family. He even listened to them open Christmas presents through his bedroom wall. It wasn't until Easter Sunday that his father allowed him to leave his room. Bo walked out of that room a different person, and his life didn't get any easier during the next eight years. He isn't referred to as Ironman for nothing.

Curriculum Connections: Health, Physical Education

Crutcher titles this book *Ironman* because Bo is an "ironman" both psychologically and physically. Have students design their own multitype competition in class, choosing the types of events they want to include. As they choose the events for the competition, have them research the muscle groups that are most used by each, and have them try to design a competition with events that will use all the main groups of muscles.

Crutcher, Chris, *Staying Fat for Sarah Byrnes.*

HarperCollins, 1993, 224pp. $15.95. ISBN: 0-688-1152-7. Bantam Doubleday Dell, 1995, 216pp. $4.99. ISBN: 0-440-21906-X

Subjects: Child Abuse, Fathers and Daughters, Friendship, High Schools, Swimming, Weight Control
Genres: Realistic, Sports
Lists: 2000 B of BBYA, 1999 PP
Levels: BL 7–12, SLJ 8 & Up

Annotation: Overweight Eric "Moby" Calhoune, and Sarah Byrnes, who is badly scarred by facial burns, have been friends since junior high school. When Eric begins losing weight because he is on the swim team, he tries to gain it back so he can stay friends with Sarah. When Sarah stops talking and is hospitalized in a psychiatric ward, Eric begins to investigate why, and discovers that her father had intentionally burned her as a child.

Booktalk: Eric told the psychiatric ward nurse that she had to use her full name—Sarah Byrnes. Those junior high idiots had thought they were so smart when they figured out the pun between Sarah's last name and her disfiguring facial burns. So Sarah saved herself the hassles and insisted on being referred to by her whole name. When the nurse was gone, Eric whispered *Crispy Pork Rinds* into Sarah Byrnes' ear. Sarah Byrnes was crispy, Eric was a porker, and the rinds were the parts no one pays any attention to. There was no reaction. Eric knew Sarah Byrnes was buried deep inside herself when even the reference to the underground school newspaper named after them didn't bring a response.

Dickinson, Peter, *Eva.*

Bantam Doubleday Dell, 1990, 219pp. $4.99. ISBN: 0-440-20766-5

Subjects: Accidents, Medical Experimentation, Parent and Child, Survival
Genre: Science Fiction
Lists: 1994 B of BBYA, 2000 B of BBYA, 1999 PP
Levels: BL 7–12, SLJ 8–12

Annotation: Fourteen-year-old Eva had been in a car accident. Her functioning brain was transplanted into the body of a chimpanzee, but the instincts and subconscious memories of the chimpanzee are still there. Eva has to deal with the media coverage of her new life and eventually dies in the forest to which she escapes with other chimps.

Booktalk: Eva remembers being at the beach with her parents and the chimps, and that is all she remembers until she wakes up in the hospital and can't feel or move her body. Her parents are exhausted, and the look on her mother's face is scary. Something has to be terribly wrong, and Eva is sure it has something to do with the accident and her. She tries to close one eye and look at her nose with the other. But there isn't a nose there. That's when she insists she look at herself in a mirror. She knows from the horrified look on her mother's face that she is not going to like what she sees.

Curriculum Connection: Health Science

Eva was published in 1988. It is considered a science fiction novel, in other words, a story that could become reality in the future. Do we have the medical and technological ability to do the type of transplant that occurred in this novel? Are there ethical considerations that should be taken into account? What types of transplants take place today that were not possible in 1988?

34 Draper, Sharon M., *Darkness Before Dawn.*

Atheneum, 2001, 233pp. $16. ISBN: 0-689-83080-7
Subjects: African Americans, High Schools, Rape, Track and Field
Genres: Multicultural, Realistic
List: Author's Choice
Level: SLJ 9 & Up

Annotation: Against her parents' wishes, 18-year-old Keisha gets involved with the smooth-talking college-age track coach as she tries to deal with her boyfriend's suicide. After the prom, she sneaks out for a late dinner with him and finds herself with a knife at her throat as he tries to rape her. She gets away after she cuts his face with the knife. Companion novel to *Forged by Fire* (Atheneum, 1997) and *Tears of a Tiger* (Atheneum, 1994).

Booktalk: As Keisha stepped forward to give her speech at the graduation ceremony, her legs began to shake and her mind flashed back through the last year. Her boyfriend, Andy, had committed suicide, and Keisha was feeling lost and lonely in her circle of friends. That's when smooth-talking Jonathan entered her life. He was the principal's son, a junior in college, majoring in education, and observing classes and helping coach the track and basketball teams. All the girls were drooling over him, but he picked Keisha out of the group. Keisha fell under his spell and began sneaking out to spend time with him. But she found out the hard way that Jonathan was interested in more than dating her and was not about to take no for an answer. She found herself fighting for her life as he held a small silver knife to her throat. As she stepped out onto the stage at the graduation ceremony, what she had had to do to escape flashed through her mind, but she got herself under control to give her speech—ready to go on with her life.

Curriculum Connections: Health, Psychology

Have students discuss the differences and similarities between date rape and rape by a stranger, as well as date rape drugs.

Draper, Sharon M., *Forged by Fire.*

Atheneum, 1997, 151pp. $16. ISBN: 0-689-80699-X. Aladdin, 1998, 156pp. $3.99. ISBN: 0-689-81851-3
Subjects: African Americans, Basketball, Brothers and Sisters, Child Sexual Abuse, Stepfamilies
Genres: Multicultural, Realistic
Lists: 2002 PP, 1998 BBYA, 1998 QP
Award: Coretta Scott King
Levels: BL 7–10, SLJ 7–10

Annotation: Seventeen-year-old Gerald is back with his mother after she served jail time for leaving him alone as a young child when he set fire to the apartment. His mother returns with another child, Angel, four years younger than he, and a stepfather who abuses her. It is difficult to concentrate on school and basketball when he feels he is responsible for keeping Angel safe. Companion novel to *Darkness Before Dawn* (Atheneum, 2001) and *Tears of a Tiger* (Atheneum, 1994).

Booktalk: Gerald had a wonderful life with his great aunt until his mother got out of prison and insisted he live with her instead of his beloved aunt. Things would be very different because his mother had a new man in her life and a daughter named Angel. Angel was a shy, pretty child, so the name appeared to suit her, but in reality Gerald should have been the child named Angel because he was his little sister's guardian angel, protecting her from an abusive father. Gerald thought that they were safe when Angel's father was put in prison, but he got out again. Soon Gerald would face his two greatest fears—not being able to protect Angel and a childhood fear of fire.

36 Draper, Sharon M., *Tears of a Tiger.*

Atheneum, 1994, 192pp. $16. ISBN: 0-689-31878-2. Aladdin, 1996, 180pp. $3.95. ISBN: 0-689-80698-1
Subjects: Accidents, African Americans, Authorship, Basketball, Death, High Schools, Letter Writing, Suicide
Genres: Multicultural, Realistic
Lists: 2000 B of BBYA, 1996 BBYA
Levels: BL 7–10, SLJ 9 & Up

Annotation: Andy Jackson was driving the car the night Robert Washington was killed in the accident. He and his basketball teammates and friends at school react to Robert's death through letters, poems, prayers, and phone calls. Companion novel to *Darkness Before Dawn* (Atheneum, 2001) and *Forged by Fire* (Atheneum, 1997).

Booktalk: Andy doesn't feel like he has any other way out. He knows he had been drinking that night, and there was no excuse for the accident. All he can think about is Robert sitting next to him, with his feet up on the dashboard. If he hadn't had his feet on the dashboard, he wouldn't have gotten pinned in the car. Andy can still see Robert's legs and feet sticking out through the windshield and hear his screams as the car caught fire. How is he supposed to live with that? He sees how everyone is looking at him. The guilt is eating him alive. For Andy, there is no other way out. He heads for his bedroom.

Curriculum Connections: English, Psychology
   Read aloud excerpts from the book in class. The chapters are short and consist of letters, dialogue between students or teachers, newspaper clippings, and prayers. Have students either discuss the chapters, or in the case of a letter, respond to it in writing.

37 Duncan, Lois, *I Know What You Did Last Summer.*

Simon & Schuster, 1975, 198pp. $4.99. ISBN: 0-671-01722-5
Subjects: Accidents, Brothers, Friendship, Murder
Genre: Mystery, Realistic
List: Author's Choice
Levels: No current interest levels available

Annotation: Two young couples hit and kill a boy on a bicycle and don't report the accident. Later the boy's stepbrother, who has returned from Vietnam, stalks them.

Booktalk: Julie was the first one in their group to get a note that read I KNOW WHAT YOU DID LAST SUMMER. Opening the envelope and seeing those words scared her so badly that her legs felt like rubber and she couldn't walk. She didn't tell anyone about the note because Barry had convinced the group not to tell anyone about what had happened that summer night. He was too wrapped up in himself to care about how anyone else felt. He was too selfish to feel guilty for what they did. But Barry was about to pay for his selfishness. He stepped out of the fraternity house, trying to adjust his eyes to the darkness, when a flash as bright as a flare went off in front of his face. The next thing he knew, he felt a terrible piercing pain in his stomach and spine. Someone *did* know what they had done last summer and was seeking revenge.

Curriculum Connection: English

Many novels have been made into movies. Students may think that by watching the movie they "know" the story. Have students choose a novel that has a movie version. Have them read the novel, then watch the movie. Ask them to compare the book and the movie, discussing how the plot or characters were changed for the movie and what is missing from the movie. Did they like the book or movie better, and why? For example, the movie based on *I Know What You Did Last Summer* is different from the book.

Ferris, Jean, *Love Among the Walnuts.*

38

Harcourt Brace, 1998, 216pp. $16. ISBN: 0-15-201590-6. Penguin Putnam, 2001, 224pp. $5.99. ISBN: 0-14-131009-5
Subjects: The Elderly, Mental Illness, Parent and Child
Genres: Humor, Mystery
List: 1999 BBYA
Levels: SLJ 7 & Up, VOYA 7–12

Annotation: The wealthy Huntingtons raise their son, Sandy, on a remote estate. All is right in their small, isolated world until Sandy's greedy uncles try to kill his parents. The plan goes awry, and Sandy and the chauffeur figure out what the uncles gave his parents that put them into a coma, with the help of their neighbors, the not-so-crazy residents of Walnut Manor.

Booktalk: All the wealthy Horatio and Mousy Huntington wanted out of life was to raise their son, Alexander (Sandy), in a safe environment. Raised in isolation, Sandy has no clue how to deal with his two wicked uncles, who have somehow put his parents into a coma, or the romantic feelings he has when he is around the beautiful, blonde nurse who has come to take care of them. Things get even stranger when Sandy involves the wacky residents of Walnut Manor, the mental institution next door, in solving the mystery of how Bart and Bernie produced his parents' catatonic state.

39 Fleischman, Paul, *Mind's Eye.*

Holt, 1999, 108pp. $15.95. ISBN: 0-8050-6314-5. Bantam Doubleday Dell, 2001, 112pp. $5.50. ISBN: 0-440-22901-4
Subjects: The Elderly, Physically Handicapped
Genre: Realistic
List: 2000 BBYA
Levels: BL 8–12, SLJ 8 & Up

Annotation: When sixteen-year-old Courtney is paralyzed in a horseback riding accident, she is placed in a nursing home. She becomes friends with an elderly woman who takes her on imaginary journeys via books and her mind. Formatted as a play.

Booktalk: Courtney is trying to escape into sleep so she doesn't have to deal with where she is, when she hears a persistent female voice. The voice is telling her that she is going to have to figure out how to remake herself, that instead of spending hours on her hair and how she looks, Courtney has to quit acting like a typical teenager and learn how to fly through the sixth window. To do that, she has to learn how to use her imagination; it is the only way she will ever feel free again. Courtney is about to tell the old woman to be quiet when she hears her say that she has a plan for getting both of them out of there. Courtney opens her eyes and begins to listen.

Curriculum Connection: English

This novel is written in play form. In other words, it is all dialogue. Have students imagine that they are lying paralyzed in a nursing home with an elderly roommate. Their stepfather has just come to visit for the first time since putting them in the nursing home after he said he could not take care of them anymore. Have students write the dialogue between the two of them when they tell their stepfather how they feel about being institutionalized.

40 Fraustino, Lisa Rowe, *Ash.*

Orchard, 1995, 171pp. $16.95. ISBN: 0-531-08739-5
Subjects: Brothers, Family Problems, Letter Writing, Mental Illness
Genre: Realistic
Lists: 1996 BBYA, 1996 QP
Levels: BL 9–12, SLJ 8 & Up

Annotation: Via letters, 15-year-old Wes chronicles the descent into schizophrenia by his 18-year-old brother, Ash, and how his manic behavior affects their rural Maine family. The family thinks Ash is into drugs until a suicide attempt results in a proper diagnosis.

Booktalk: It all began when my brother Ash hit a moose doing 80 on the way home from my violin lessons. But he really went off the deep end about a month later at my birthday party when he came out singing "Happy Birthday" with nothing on but his electric guitar, and said things to my best friend about his sister and mother. That set the whole bunch of us off into saying terrible things to each other, and my best friend Merle hasn't spoken to me since. It's now a year later, Wes is in a coma, and the doctors are telling us that he is schizophrenic. All Dad can say is he should have taken him to the hospital when he whacked out at my birthday. And all I can do is write Ash letters. Here they are. I am ready for you to read them now.

Curriculum Connections: Health, Psychology

Read excerpts from the book in which Ash's schizophrenia has control of him. Discuss with students how disconcerting and frightening this is for his younger brother, Wes. Schizophrenia is not a well-understood mental illness. Have students research this illness, using at least one recent medical journal article that discusses what causes schizophrenia and how it is treated. Using their knowledge of this illness, have them write Wes a letter to help him understand his older brother's illness.

French, Albert, *Billy.*

Viking Penguin, 1995, 224pp. $12.95. ISBN: 0-140-17908-9
Subjects: African Americans, Murder, Race Relations
Genres: Historical, Multicultural
List: Author's Choice
Level: Adult

Annotation: In 1937, blacks and whites lived on opposite sides of the tracks in Banes, Mississippi. When 10-year-old Billy and his friend crossed the tracks to wade in a white family's pond, they were beat up by two teenage girls. Billy fought back, accidentally killing the 15-year-old white girl, and was later executed as an adult.

Booktalk: We have problems with racial prejudice today, but back in the 1930s it was much worse, especially in the South. Ten-year-old Billy and his friend cross the tracks to the white side of town and are caught wading in the Pasko's pond. Lori Pasko, a mean-spirited 15-year-old, sneaks up on Billy and beats him up. Billy pulls a knife from his pocket and fights back, stabbing her in the chest. Lori dies and the sheriff has to keep the white side of town from lynching little Billy. But what happens to Billy is as horrific as a lynching. Ten-year-old Billy is arrested for murder and tried as an adult. In 1937, in Mississippi, the death penalty was enforced, and the form of execution was by electric chair.

Curriculum Connections: Government, History

After sharing what happened to Billy with students, ask them to discuss whether they think a black person could have gotten a fair trial in Mississippi in the 1930s. Have them research what the South was like in relation to integration prior to the Civil Rights Movement. Also, have them discuss what happened to Billy in relation to the current trend in the United States to try juvenile offenders as adults. At what age should a juvenile be considered an adult in a court of law?

42 Gilbert, Barbara Snow, *Stone Water.*

Front Street, 1996, 169pp. $15.95. ISBN: 1-886910-11-1. Bantam Doubleday Dell, 1998, 176pp. $4.50. ISBN: 0-440-22755-0

Subjects: Death, The Elderly, Grandparents, Suicide
Genre: Realistic
List: Author's Choice
Levels: BL 5–9, SLJ 6–10

Annotation: Fifteen-year-old Grant Hughes is close to his grandfather and spends time with him on his ranch. When his grandfather has a massive stroke and is put in a nursing home, Grant opens the letter his grandfather wrote to him and has to decide whether to help his grandfather die.

Booktalk: Grant's parents are too busy to really care about what happens to his grandfather. They rarely visited him on his ranch and after he had a massive stroke, they put him in a nursing home. Grant knows his rancher grandfather hates being trapped inside his useless body. When the grandfather goes into a coma, Grant opens the letter his grandfather left him. Inside is a story about an Indian Chief and a young brave who helps the old Indian Chief die with dignity. His grandfather also leaves Grant a message saying that if he understands what the story means, he is man enough to help his grandfather. Grant now holds his grandfather's life in his hands. Can he live with himself if he helps his grandfather die? Can he live with himself if he doesn't? Life doesn't always leave us with easy choices.

Curriculum Connections: Health, Psychology

Euthanasia raises legal, ethical, and religious questions. Divide the class in two groups, with one group doing research to support euthanasia and the other group researching information against euthanasia. After the research part of the assignment, have the two groups choose group leaders and engage in a class debate on the two sides of this issue.

43

Gilstrap, John, *Nathan's Run.*

Warner Books, 1996, 368pp. $6.99. ISBN: 0-446-60468-2
Subjects: Child Abuse, Murder
Genre: Mystery, Realistic
Lists: 2000 PP, 1997 BBYA
Level: Adult

Annotation: Twelve-year-old Nathan is on the run after escaping from a juvenile detention center, where he killed one of the guards in self-defense. He calls a radio talk show host to tell his side of the story and to get help, as he eludes a hired killer.

Booktalk: Mark Bailey sat cross-legged on the sofa, with only the stove light and the television on. On a night like this, he needed to be in the dark. He didn't want to be seen. He knew he was probably going to go to hell for this, but he just wanted the dirty business with Nathan done and over with so he could get on with the rest of his life. He was waiting for the 11 o'clock news, waiting for the newscaster to report that 12-year-old Nathan Bailey had been stabbed to death in the Juvenile Detention Center. But the news report brought Mark Bailey to the floor. Instead, the reporter said that a supervisor had been found slain and that the suspected killer was a 12-year-old boy. Street-smart Mark Bailey wasn't going to survive this get-rich scheme. Nor did he think his nephew would. The next guy sent after Nathan wouldn't be so stupid.

Curriculum Connection: Government
   In the United States a person is supposedly considered innocent until proven guilty, but in Nathan's case he is considered guilty until proven innocent. Have students research recent criminal cases involving teenagers. Do the media or the lawyers depict them as "innocent" or "guilty" prior to the jury's decision?

44

Glovach, Linda, *Beauty Queen.*

HarperCollins, 1998, 169pp. $14.95. ISBN: 0-06-205161-X
Subjects: Death, Drug Abuse, Journal Writing
Genre: Realistic
Lists: 2000 YAC, 1999 QP
Levels: SLJ 10 & Up, VOYA 10–12

Annotation: Nineteen-year-old Sam moves out of the house of her alcoholic mother and lecherous boyfriend to an apartment of her own, thinking that life will get better. But she ends up dancing topless to pay her rent. Sam chronicles her heroin use in her diary, right up to her fatal overdose.

Booktalk: Sam couldn't make enough money at Chicken & Ribs to move out, but she didn't want to deal with her alcoholic mother and that lecherous boyfriend of hers every time she came home from work. Then her friend Nicole heard about how much money they could make as topless dancers. Sam didn't think they'd get hired, but they did. Now Sam has to figure out how she is going to go out there and take her top off in front of a crowd of men. Even the shots of tequila aren't working. It isn't until Widow, the biker chick, offers to help her out and the needle works its way into her vein and the rush warms her up from head to toe, that she feels confident enough to get up on that stage. That first bite of heroin would prove to be more deadly than the bite of a black widow spider.

Curriculum Connection: Health

Sam thinks that she will not become addicted because she is skin-popping the heroin. Have students research the psychological effects of drug use and how addicts convince themselves that they do not have an addiction.

45 Goldman, E. M., *Getting Lincoln's Goat: An Elliot Armbruster Mystery.*

Bantam Doubleday Dell, 1997, 224pp. $3.99. ISBN: 0-440-41332-X
Subjects: High Schools, Occupations
Genres: Humor, Mystery
List: 1996 BBYA
Levels: BL 7–10, SLJ 6–10

Annotation: Fifteen-year-old Elliot wants to be a private detective. When Lincoln the goat, the school's mascot, comes up missing, he takes the case. Elliott, along with some help from his friends, has a chance to try out his investigative skills by following leads as to the goat's whereabouts.

Booktalk: Elliot knew he should have just said he wanted to be a history teacher and been done with it when it was his turn. Mr. Hardy, the history teacher, didn't like to have his time wasted, so instead of going through an interview like he was supposed to, he had a handout he gave to students who chose history teacher as their occupation to research. But not Elliot—before he knew it, he had blurted out his intended occupation: private eye. Now, you have to understand that Elliot truly wants to be a private investigator, but now he has to do the assignment in relation to becoming a private investigator. Where is Elliot going to find a real private eye to interview for a school assignment? He can't very well just call up a private detective listed in the phone book and ask if he can interview him for a school assignment. Or can he?

Curriculum Connection: Career Education

When Elliot and his fellow students choose the occupations they will research, many of them pick occupations based on family expectations. Bruno truly doesn't want to become a carpenter, but all of the men in his family work in the family business. Francie really wants to explore the Amazon, not become a trial attorney like her mother. Read aloud this section of the book and discuss realistic expectations of a career, as well as how one can deal with family expectations concerning careers in which a student has no interest.

46

Grant, Cynthia D., *Mary Wolf.*

Atheneum, 1995, 166pp, $16. ISBN: 0-689-80007-X. Simon & Schuster, 1997, 256pp. $4.99. ISBN: 0-689-81251-5
Subjects: Death, Family Problems, Fathers and Daughters
Genre: Realistic
Lists: 1999 PP, 1996 BBYA
Levels: BL 7–12, SLJ 6–10

Annotation: Sixteen-year-old Mary Wolf tries to keep her family together as they aimlessly travel the country in the family motor home after her father loses his job and their home. When the motor home breaks down and her father loses control, Mary has to save her family.

Booktalk: I have had enough. Daddy is on a rampage again because I suggested we go back to Nebraska so he could find a job. I told him that it wasn't the end of the world that he lost his stupid job. There are other jobs out there. He got furious. You'd think I would have known to shut up at that point, but I was on a roll. I told him what I thought about the kids sitting in the motor home, watching TV all day instead of going to school, and about Mama stealing stuff from everywhere we stopped. The next thing I knew I was flat on my back in the sand with the side of my face burning from the slap and Daddy screaming at me that I had made him hit me by ruining what had been a perfectly good day. His temper was getting worse and the outbursts more violent. As I got up from the ground, I knew things were not going to get better; they were going to get worse, just like Daddy's drinking had.

Curriculum Connections: Psychology, Sociology

Mary Wolf's family is not homeless, because they have a motor home to live in, but there are families living in homeless shelters in the United States. Have students research the percentage of the homeless who are families, rather than the stereotypical single male or female street person teens may associate with the term "homeless." What impact does being homeless have on the children in a family?

47 Grant, Cynthia D., *The White Horse.*

Atheneum, 1998, 157pp. $16. ISBN: 0-689-82127-1. Aladdin, 2000, 160pp. $4.99. ISBN: 0-689-83263-X
Subjects: Drug Abuse, Family Problems, Mothers and Daughters, Pregnancy, Teachers
Genre: Realistic
List: 1999 QP
Levels: BL 9–12, SLJ 8 & Up, VOYA 6–12

Annotation: In her English assignments, 16-year-old Raina chronicles her life with a drug-addicted mother and boyfriend and her pregnancy. When a desperate Raina asks her teacher for help, the teacher adopts both Raina and the baby.

Booktalk: Raina listened as Granny and her mother relived the past. Her mother wanted more out of life, but she got pregnant and Granny wouldn't let her have an abortion or give the baby up for adoption. Her mother bemoaned the fact that she didn't have a graduation picture in the high school yearbook. Raina couldn't help but laugh inside and think about what she would have written next to her mother's graduation picture: "Hopes to have seven children and make them miserable." She certainly had accomplished that, at least in Raina's case. But Raina would discover that life wasn't any easier out on the streets with her heroin-addicted boyfriend, Sonny, than at home with her mother. Raina kept getting skinnier and her belly kept getting bigger. Was that old saying, "Like mother, like daughter," true in relation to Raina and her mother?

48 Grimes, Nikki, *Jazmin's Notebook.*

Dial, 1998, 102pp. $15.99. ISBN: 0-8037-2224-9. Penguin Putnam, 2000, 112pp. $4.99. ISBN: 0-14-130702-1
Subjects: African Americans, Authorship, Journal Writing, Mothers and Daughters, Sisters
Genres: Historical, Multicultural
List: Author's Choice
Award: Coretta Scott King Honor
Levels: BL 7–10, SLJ 6–10, VOYA 6–12

Annotation: Fourteen-year-old Jazmin lives with her sister in 1960s Harlem, dealing with her turbulent life, including her alcoholic mother's hospitalization in a psychiatric hospital, through writing poetry and journal entries.

Booktalk: Have you ever had your parents or grandparents embarrass you by showing people your baby pictures? Or have you ever had to bite your lip to keep from laughing out loud when a friend's grandmother showed you one of those bare-bottomed baby-on-the-rug pictures of a friend? Well, that's what happened to Jazmin. She was in the drugstore when the grandma of one of the basketball players was bragging on his prom picture. That wasn't bad, but then the grandma pulled out a picture of him as a naked baby. What is it with grown-ups always showing pictures of naked babies? Jazmin would never be able to look at that muscled, six-foot frame quite the same again. It didn't help any that she was laughing so hard that tears were streaming down her cheeks when he arrived to pick up his grandmother and immediately snatched the picture out of her hand. What is it with adults and baby pictures, anyway?

Curriculum Connection: English

Although Jazmin laughed when she saw the baby pictures of one of the guys at school, she also was jealous. There weren't any baby pictures of her for her older sister to share with anyone because Jazmin had spent many years in foster homes. Jazmin decided that instead of photographs she would create pictures with her pen—she wrote about her experiences. Have students write a "snapshot" essay about a humorous or memorable experience from their childhood, making it as clear and colorful as possible, with appropriate adjectives and descriptive writing.

49

Haddix, Margaret Peterson, *Don't You Dare Read This, Mrs. Dunphrey.*

Simon & Schuster, 1996, 108pp, $15. ISBN: 0-689-80097-5. Simon & Schuster, 1997, 125pp. $4.99. ISBN: 0-689-81543-3
Subjects: Brothers and Sisters, Child Abuse, Fathers and Daughters, Journal Writing, Teachers
Genre: Realistic
Lists: 1998 YAC, 1997 BBYA, 1997 QP
Levels: BL 7–10, SLJ 7 & Up

Annotation: The unstable mother of 16-year-old Tish Bonner is delighted that their long-absent father is back, but Tish knows it won't be long before the abuse starts again. Tish writes about her life in her English journal, but prefaces most entries with "Don't read this Mrs. Dunphrey." When her mother leaves, Tish tries to pay the bills and take care of her brother on her own. But eventually she has no choice but to ask Mrs. Dunphrey to read her whole journal so she can get help.

Booktalk: Tish was glad when her father left, but now he's back and so is his abusive behavior. She can't see why her mother is so frantic about having her father stay with them. He is an abusive jerk and is running up her mother's charge cards. Tish is so busy making sure her little brother, Matt, is safe that she doesn't see her mother going off the deep end when he leaves again. Can Tish handle it when she comes home to a cold, empty house to find a note from her mother stating that she has left them to go look for their father? Her mother didn't leave her any money. How is Tish going to pay the bills and how is she going to take care of Matt? And how is she going to keep anyone from knowing that their mother abandoned them?

50 Haddix, Margaret, *Turnabout.*

Simon & Schuster, 2000, 223pp. $17. ISBN: 0-689-82187-5
Subjects: The Elderly, Friendship, Medical Experimentation
Genre: Science Fiction
List: Author's Choice
Levels: SLJ 6–10, VOYA 6–12

Annotation: In the year 2000, Melly and Anny Beth, two elderly women, are selected to participate in Project Turnabout, involving an injection that will make them un-age. Eighty-five years later they are now teenagers, but cannot stop getting younger, as the shot to stop the un-aging process kills the participants. They find one of Melly's relatives to take care of them as they un-age toward birth.

Booktalk: If you were a really old person ready to die and you could un-age to be your age again, would you? It would mean reliving your life backwards, becoming younger each year. That is what happens to Melly and Anny Beth when they unwittingly become involved in a medical experiment that has gone wrong. The doctors thought the participants could pick an age they wanted to un-age to and take a second shot that would stop the un-aging process. However, the second shot has proved deadly for all who have taken it. Should Melly and Anny Beth take the shot or un-age until their birth? What happens then?

Curriculum Connections: Health, Psychology

Have students discuss whether the doctors in *Turnabout* have ethically exceeded what should be allowed in medical experimentation. What if a doctor determined what causes the aging process and was willing to sell the aging antidote to the highest bidder? What might happen?

Hahn, Mary Downing, *The Wind Blows Backward.*

Clarion, 1993, 272pp. $15. ISBN: 0-395-62975-6. Avon, 1994, 266pp. $3.99. ISBN: 0-380-77530-1

Subjects: Emotional Problems, Fathers and Sons, Relationships, Suicide
Genres: Realistic, Romance
List: Author's Choice
Levels: BL 8–12, SLJ 9–12

51

Annotation: During their senior year, quiet Lauren and Spencer, the jock, renew their middle school friendship and fall in love. But Spencer has changed. He is depressed and worries he will follow his father's suicidal footsteps.

Booktalk: Spencer had been Lauren's middle school crush. Here it was senior year and Spencer was back in Lauren's life. Lauren knew exactly when she fell totally in love with Spencer again. It was the night he picked up her copy of *Rain Makes Applesauce* (Holiday House, 1985), a childhood favorite of hers, and said it was one of his favorite books too. They sat on the floor and recited the lines together. They stared at each other in amazement—they both knew the same book by heart. That's when Lauren knew Spencer was her other half, her best friend, and the one she would spend the rest of her life with, if she could keep him from taking his own.

Curriculum Connection: English

Lauren and Spencer know the same children's book by heart. Have students bring their favorite children's books to class and share them with the rest of the students. Discuss how many of them bring the same titles, as well as how many titles are brought in that they never read as young children. Have the students talk or write about what element of the book made it memorable for them.

Hanauer, Cathi, *My Sister's Bones.*

Dell, 1997, 258pp. $11.95. ISBN: 0-385-31704-2

Subjects: Eating Disorders, Fathers and Daughters, Jewish Americans, Sexual Relationships, Sisters
Genres: Multicultural, Realistic
List: 1997 BBYA
Level: Adult

52

Annotation: Fifteen-year-old Billie is dealing with a domineering Jewish father, a boyfriend on the wrestling team, and the effect her older sister's anorexia is having on the family.

Booktalk: Control is the bottom line in Billie's family, and her father has it. As a surgeon, he demands the best from himself and his family, at any cost. All Billie hears about are her grades and her SAT scores. But he's losing control of her older sister, Cassie. Billie can see it. The university called and asked them to come get Cassie. She isn't eating and she has given all her clothes away to charity. She drags around the house in a too-big pair of sweatpants and sweatshirt, with a vacant look in her eyes. But he keeps pushing, pushing his girls to be the best they can be, no matter what the cost is to them. Billie can see what it's costing Cassie, and she doesn't know what to do. How much is his love and approval going to cost her? Can she handle the cost, or will she try to escape like Cassie?

Curriculum Connections: Career Education, English, Psychology

The demands parents place on students to succeed in school can be tremendous. Have students write a letter to Billie with advice on how to deal with her overbearing father's demands on her.

53 Hardman, Ric Lynden, *Sunshine Rider: The First Vegetarian Western.*

Delacorte, 1998, 352pp, $15.95. ISBN: 0-385-3254306. Bantam Doubleday Dell, 1999, 352pp. $4.99. ISBN: 0-440-22812-3

Subjects: Occupations, The Old West, Self-esteem
Genres: Historical, Humor
List: 1999 BBYA
Levels: BL 9–12, SLJ 5–9, VOYA 6–9

Annotation: Seventeen-year-old Wylie Jackson steals a horse and runs away from his first Texas cattle drive, learns natural remedies from an Indian medicine man, partners up with a "snake-oil" salesman, and eventually is taken in and trained by a real doctor. Each chapter is prefaced with recipes from the late 1800s.

Booktalk: If you ever saw the look in the eyes of a calf that is about to be shot in the head, you would become a vegetarian too. If that didn't convert you, seeing what the camp cook has to do to fry you up a steak would have you reaching for the beans instead. Here's what happens: First the steer is hit on the head with a four pound sledge, but only hard enough to stun it so that it is still alive when they hang it by the hind legs and cut its jugular vein. That way the heart pumps all the blood out. You don't even want to hear the rest of what is done to prepare that steak for your plate. Just take my word for it—I became a vegetarian while on a Texas cattle drive for very good reasons.

Curriculum Connection: Health

Wylie was a vegetarian in a time that eating beef was part of life. No one knew about cholesterol or the problems with eating too much red meat. Have students research the typical diet of a cowboy on a cattle drive, determining the nutritional content of such a diet.

Hautman, Pete, *Mr. Was.*

Simon & Schuster, 1996, 216pp. $16. ISBN: 0-689-81068-7. Simon & Schuster, 1998, 240pp. $4.99. ISBN: 0-689-81914-5
Subjects: Family Problems, Grandparents, Moving, Murder, Time Travel, War, World War II
Genres: Fantasy, Historical, Mystery
Lists: 1999 PP, 1997 BBYA
Levels: BL 8–12, SLJ 7–10

54

Annotation: Jack travels back in time through a 50-year door to 1941 in an attempt to change the past to save his mother's life in the present. Instead, he meets his grandparents and falls in love with his grandmother.

Booktalk: We moved the day before my 16th birthday. I didn't want to move, but we didn't have much choice. Like Mom said, Dad would get out of jail, but I really didn't want go back to that old house. I remembered the door and what had happened to me when I went through it. I was scared that it was real and just as scared that it wasn't. I did not want to live in that house, but Mom didn't care. She just wanted to get away from Dad and get a job. If only it could have been that easy. Of course he got out of jail, and of course he knew where to find us. At first everything was fine, and then he started drinking again. It was my baseball bat he hit her with. I heard the dull thud, but she was dead before I got down the stairs. I might be scared of that door, but I do know that if I don't walk through it, I can't journey back in time so I can stop him from killing my mother.

Curriculum Connection: History

Although *Mr. Was* is a time-travel fantasy, it is an interesting way to introduce the 1940s and World War II to students. Several times in the book, Jack gives away his future identity by referring to things not invented yet, such as the television, as well as trying to pay for something with a quarter with a 1986 date. Have the students research the 1940s in relation to the technology of that time period vs. today. What items from the 1940s are still being used?

55 Hautman, Pete, *Stone Cold.*

Simon & Schuster, 1998, 163pp. $16. ISBN: 0-689-81759-2. Simon & Schuster, 2000, 176pp. $4.99. ISBN: 0-689-83321-0
Subjects: Family Problems, Gambling
Genre: Realistic
List: 1999 QP
Levels: BL 7–12, SLJ 7 & Up, VOYA 7–12

Annotation: Sixteen-year-old Denn has a thriving landscaping business, a best friend, and a girlfriend, but becomes addicted to high stakes poker when he realizes that he can tell what the other players are thinking, while he keeps his own face expressionless. His gambling addiction results in his alienation from his family and friends.

Booktalk: Denn had everything going for him. At 16, he had his own lawn care business and lots of money in his pocket. He had a girlfriend and a great best friend. Then he started playing poker and realized he had an amazing skill. He could make his face go stone cold so the other players didn't know what kind of hand he had. He also could pick up on the other players' facial expressions and body movements that gave them away. He was making money hand over fist, but that wasn't what was keeping him in the game. All he could think about was the feel of those cool, slick cards between his fingers. Denn was addicted.

Curriculum Connection: Psychology

When we think of addictions, we usually think of drugs and alcohol. Have students research other types of addictions that are less well known, such as gambling.

56 Henry, Chad, *DogBreath Victorious.*

Holiday House, 1996, 188pp. $16.95. ISBN: 0-8234-1458-2
Subjects: Letter Writing, Mothers and Sons, Music
Genre: Humor
List: Author's Choice
Level: VOYA 7–12

Annotation: Tim Threfall's Seattle-based grunge rock band is trying to win the Rad Band Contest prize of $2,000, but his band loses to a girl band. The pain of losing becomes humiliation when he discovers that his mother is a member of the Angry Housewives, the winning band.

Booktalk: It was already the worst day of my life before I even ran into the counselor in the hallway. At lunchtime Suzie Blethins, the love of my life—she just didn't know it yet—made a barfing motion in my direction. Then I got a D- on my song "Toe Jamming."

How is that possible? I am a great musician. I tried to explain to Mrs. Lewis that the song was supposed to be repetitive, just like life and school, but she told me to write a better song. Then I encountered Mr. Thompson, the counselor, who tried to talk to me about how difficult it must have been when my dad died suddenly. I told him that my mom shouldn't have showed him the bills before dinner, but he did not appreciate my sense of humor. Instead he started talking about my bad attitude and my appearance. Now wait a minute—I have my public to think about. I am the leader of DogBreath and besides, I know I look good with my pink and black Mohawk. His babble was meaningless anyway; I am going to be a millionaire rock star before I turn 25. I had quit listening until I heard him say that I would have to quit the band if I didn't shape up my act. Quit DogBreath? No way! We were practicing for the Rad Band Contest and we were going to win that $2,000 and the recording contract! Who did he think he was anyway?

57 Hesser, Terry Spencer, *Kissing Doorknobs.*

Delacorte, 1998, 156pp. $15.95. ISBN: 0-385-32329-8. Bantam, 1999, 160pp. $4.99. ISBN: 0-440-41314-1
Subjects: Family Problems, Friendship, Mental Illness
Genre: Realistic
Lists: 1999 BBYA, 1999 QP
Levels: BL 6–12, SLJ 6 & Up, VOYA 7–12

Annotation: Fourteen-year-old Tara's obsessive-compulsive disorder has her repeating rituals over and over, such as counting the cracks in the sidewalk on the way to school. It takes over her life until she eventually receives the proper diagnosis and medical care.

Booktalk: Have you ever heard the saying, "Step on a crack, break your mother's back?" After hearing it for the first time, did you actually believe if you stepped on one of those cracks something would happen to your mother? Well, Tara does. She has what is called obsessive-compulsive disorder, which makes her count the cracks in the sidewalk, as well as be afraid to look up long enough to cross the street safely for fear she will step on a crack. Her obsession with the cracks in the sidewalks gets worse. Every day she has to count the cracks on the way to school, all 480 chances for her to do bodily harm to her mother. And if anyone interrupts her, she has to run back home to start the process all over again. Tara is beginning to feel like the sidewalk—like she is cracking.

Curriculum Connections: Health, Psychology

The character in this book, Tara, has a disorder that few people understand, even doctors, which is evident from the number of times Tara was misdiagnosed. The afterword includes a resources section with a list of organizations to contact and publications on obsessive-compulsive disorder. Have students either contact one of the organizations for further information or use one of the print resources to research this disorder.

58 Hewett, Lorri, *Dancer.*

Dutton, 1999, 214pp. $15.99. ISBN: 0-525-45968-5. Puffin, 2001, 224pp. $5.99. ISBN: 0-141-131085-5

Subjects: African Americans, Dancing, Race Relations
Genres: Multicultural, Realistic
List: 2000 BBYA
Levels: BL 7–10, VOYA 6–12

Annotation: Sixteen-year-old Stephanie struggles with her parents' concerns over her goal of becoming a world-class ballerina—a difficult feat for an African-American dancer—and her attachment to retired black dancer Miss Winnie and her nephew Vance.

Booktalk: Can you believe my dad told me I was being overly dramatic? Me? I'm the one who never misses school, and he is having a fit about missing one day. I really do think he wants me to fail. He keeps telling me that my chances as a dancer are slim. Both my parents want me to quit. They say I am spending too much time with Miss Winnie. But she understands me; they don't. One way or the other I *am* going to dance with the company on Wednesday and see the Dance Theater of Harlem perform that night. My parents are such a pain!

Curriculum Connection: History

African Americans have had a place in the world of dance, including ballet. Have students research African-American dancers and the impact they have had on the evolution of dance in the United States.

59 Hewett, Lorri, *Lives of Our Own.*

Dutton, 1998, 214pp. $15.99. ISBN: 0-525-45959-6. Penguin Putnam, 2000, 224pp. $5.99. ISBN: 0-14-130589-4

Subjects: African Americans, High Schools, Race Relations
Genres: Multicultural, Realistic
List: 2000 YAC
Levels: BL 6–9, SLJ 7–10, VOYA 10–12

Annotation: Shawna and her father return to his conservative Georgia hometown after her parents' divorce, where she discovers a link with Kari, one of the popular white girls. Shawna's African-American father and Kari's mother had been discovered together as teenagers. The two girls travel to Kari's aunts, thinking that her mother had a baby years ago.

Booktalk: When Shawna moved from Denver to Georgia, she immediately offended many of the white students with her school newspaper editorial suggesting that it was time the Old South Ball was "gone with the wind." A black girl making comments about the white girls in their long dresses and the white boys in their gray uniforms from the War of Northern Aggression didn't go over well. Having lived in this town all of her life, Kari truly didn't know what Shawna's problem was—many of the other towns nearby had separate proms for black and white students too. Kari liked the idea of clinging to old traditions; she had grown up hearing about the Spring Ball all of her life. Her grandmother had been crowned Belle of the Ball when she was in high school. Who did this black girl think she was anyway? Kari let some of her anger fly, right along with a rock that smashed through the front window of Shawna's grandmother's house.

Curriculum Connection: History

Kari and her family refer to the Civil War as the War of Northern Aggression. Have students research Southern attitudes toward the Civil War. How do they differ from the attitudes of Northerners?

Hobbs, Valerie, *Get It While It's Hot. Or Not.* 60

Orchard, 1996, 182pp. $17.99. ISBN: 0-531-08890-1. Morrow/Avon, 1998, 192pp. $3.99. ISBN: 0-380-73101-0
Subjects: Authorship, Friendship, Mothers and Daughters, Pregnancy
Genre: Realistic
List: 1998 YAC
Levels: BL 9–12, SLJ 7–10

Annotation: Megan, Kit, Mia, and Elaine made a pact to be friends till the end. The responsibility of this pact lies heavy on 16-year-old Megan's shoulders as she goes against her parents' wishes by cutting classes to help take care of pregnant Kit.

Booktalk: When one of her best friends becomes pregnant, Megan decides to write a feature story for the school newspaper on teenage sex. After gathering data, and interviewing students and the leader of a group of mothers determined to stop the distribution of condoms to teens, Megan submits the article for publication. The principal turns it down. He thinks it is too controversial for a school newspaper. But after learning that the father of her friend's unborn baby is HIV positive, Megan decides that this information is too important to not distribute. So she takes matters into her own hands. She makes copies of her article with her own money and stuffs it in student lockers and under classroom doors. Would you have learned something from Megan's article?

Curriculum Connection: Health

Teenage sexuality is an uncomfortable topic of discussion for adults. Megan interviews students and parents as to their position on condom distribution to teens. Divide the class into two teams to research condom distribution in high schools, with teams taking a stand on each side of this issue. Each team will be prepared to defend their stand during a debate.

61 Hobbs, Valerie, *How Far Would You Have Gotten If I Hadn't Called You Back?*

Orchard, 1995, 306pp. $19.95. ISBN: 0-531-09480-4
Subjects: Automobile Driving, Death, Moving, Music, Relationships, Suicide
Genres: Historical, Romance
List: 1996 BBYA
Level: SLJ 9 & Up

Annotation: It's the 1960s and 16-year-old Bron falls in love with drag racing and a young rancher when her family moves from New Jersey to Ojala, California. However, her love of the fast life involving cars destroys their relationship.

Booktalk: Usually when you think of drag racing, you think of guys and fast cars, not girls and fast cars. But when Bron saw the midnight blue beauty and slid into the leather driver's seat, she knew she wanted that car more than she wanted anything else in her whole life. It cost Bron her life's savings and a promise of part of her waitress tips each week, but Frieda let her take it that day. With the keys in her hand, she could get away from everything, at least for a while. She couldn't wait to cruise the strip.

Curriculum Connection: Career Education

Bron likes cars and even learns how to work on her car. Auto mechanics is typically thought of as a male occupation. This is a career stereotype. So is the idea that an attendant on an airplane is female. Today many flight attendants are male. Have students discuss careers in relation to gender stereotyping and the progress that has been made in the last 50 years in relation to these stereotypes.

Howe, James, *The Watcher.*

Atheneum, 1997, 173pp. $15. ISBN: 0-689-80186-6. Aladdin, 2001, 192pp. $4.99. ISBN: 0-689-83533-7
Subjects: Authorship, Child Abuse, Family Problems
Genre: Realistic
List: 1998 BBYA
Levels: BL 8–12, SLJ 7–9, VOYA 6–9

62

Annotation: A lonely, abused, 13-year-old girl sits and watches the beach, wishing she were a part of Evan's family life on the beach and that of the lifeguard Chris, who she pretends is her guardian angel.

Booktalk: She sat on the top of the wooden steps to the beach and watched. It was the first time they had let her go out by herself since they rented the beach house. She watched Evan play with his little sister and pretended they were her family. She watched Chris, the lifeguard, and wished that he could really be her guardian angel, not just the one she wrote about in the stories that filled her notebook. She came back day after day, wrapping herself up in her stories of the life she wished she had, a life without the Beast. But her real world, where the Beast roared and the music blared, was about to collide with the real people she had created a life with in her make-believe world.

Curriculum Connection: English

This novel is written from three perspectives, that of the abused girl, the boy at the beach with his family, and the lifeguard who watches over the beach. They are all looking at the same beach, but they see it differently, based on their own lives and personal concerns. Have students take a scene from a book or a short story, and write it from a different character's perspective.

Howe, Norma, *Adventures of Blue Avenger.*

Holt, 1999, 230pp. $15.95. ISBN: 0-8050-6062-6. HarperCollins, 2000, 240pp. $6.95. ISBN: 0-06-447225-6
Subjects: Death, Fathers and Sons, High Schools, Relationships
Genres: Humor, Realistic
List: 2000 BBYA
Levels: SLJ 7 & Up, VOYA 7–9

63

Annotation: After his father dies, 16-year-old David decides to become Blue Avenger, the comic book hero he created. Blue becomes the champion of the underdog. Companion novel to *Blue Avenger Cracks the Code* (Holt, 2000).

Booktalk: A double-dip rocky road ice cream cone and a tiny brown spider changed David Schumacher's life forever. If Officer Schumacher hadn't decided to stop for an ice cream cone on his way home from the police station and that little spider hadn't decided to cross the windshield of the other car and distract the driver, the two cars would not have been in proximity of each other and the accident wouldn't have happened. But it did. Three years later, on his 16th birthday, David, the son of Officer Schumacher, announces to his mother and to the school counselor that he has decided to officially change his name to Blue Avenger, the name of the comic book character he had begun to draw right after his father's death. David—oops, Blue Avenger—goes to school in his father's blue fishing vest and a blue towel tied on his head to begin his new life as the defender of the underdog. Do you think his new look will be noticed?

Curriculum Connection: Psychology

Students deal with peer pressure on a daily basis in high school. Have students discuss Blue Avenger's unusual attire and how he would be treated if he showed up in their school hallway dressed in this manner.

64 Howe, Norma, *Blue Avenger Cracks the Code.*

Holt, 2000, 296pp. $17. ISBN: 0-8050-6372-2
Subjects: Authorship, High Schools
Genres: Humor, Mystery, Realistic
List: Author's Choice
Levels: SLJ 7 & Up, VOYA 7–12

Annotation: Sixteen-year-old David, known as Blue Avenger, first helps his girlfriend find her father and then visits Venice, trying to solve the mystery of who wrote the plays and sonnets attributed to Shakespeare. Companion novel to *The Adventures of Blue Avenger* (Holt, 1999).

Booktalk: Blue Avenger figured out the mystery of why the absent father of his girlfriend, Omaha Brown, visits Rome every year to see Giordano Bruno. It didn't seem possible since Bruno, a 16th century philosopher and heretic, had been burned at the stake by the Inquisition in the year 1600. But while reading a travel guide to Rome, Blue found a reference to the gathering of Giordano Bruno followers at the foot of his statue each year. Blue knew how important it was to Omaha to see and talk to her father, so he had to figure out how to get her to Rome in three days' time. She had to be at the base of Bruno's statue on February 17th, exactly when her father would be there. Why was David, or I should say Blue Avenger, doing this? Well, that's because he was the defender of the underdog and besides, Omaha was his girlfriend. The story doesn't end there. Blue goes to Rome too, and while he is there he sets out to solve an age-old mystery of authorship.

Howe, James, *The Watcher*. 62

Atheneum, 1997, 173pp. $15. ISBN: 0-689-80186-6. Aladdin, 2001, 192pp. $4.99. ISBN: 0-689-83533-7
Subjects: Authorship, Child Abuse, Family Problems
Genre: Realistic
List: 1998 BBYA
Levels: BL 8–12, SLJ 7–9, VOYA 6–9

Annotation: A lonely, abused, 13-year-old girl sits and watches the beach, wishing she were a part of Evan's family life on the beach and that of the lifeguard Chris, who she pretends is her guardian angel.

Booktalk: She sat on the top of the wooden steps to the beach and watched. It was the first time they had let her go out by herself since they rented the beach house. She watched Evan play with his little sister and pretended they were her family. She watched Chris, the lifeguard, and wished that he could really be her guardian angel, not just the one she wrote about in the stories that filled her notebook. She came back day after day, wrapping herself up in her stories of the life she wished she had, a life without the Beast. But her real world, where the Beast roared and the music blared, was about to collide with the real people she had created a life with in her make-believe world.

Curriculum Connection: English
   This novel is written from three perspectives, that of the abused girl, the boy at the beach with his family, and the lifeguard who watches over the beach. They are all looking at the same beach, but they see it differently, based on their own lives and personal concerns. Have students take a scene from a book or a short story, and write it from a different character's perspective.

Howe, Norma, *Adventures of Blue Avenger*. 63

Holt, 1999, 230pp. $15.95. ISBN: 0-8050-6062-6. HarperCollins, 2000, 240pp. $6.95. ISBN: 0-06-447225-6
Subjects: Death, Fathers and Sons, High Schools, Relationships
Genres: Humor, Realistic
List: 2000 BBYA
Levels: SLJ 7 & Up, VOYA 7–9

Annotation: After his father dies, 16-year-old David decides to become Blue Avenger, the comic book hero he created. Blue becomes the champion of the underdog. Companion novel to *Blue Avenger Cracks the Code* (Holt, 2000).

Booktalk: A double-dip rocky road ice cream cone and a tiny brown spider changed David Schumacher's life forever. If Officer Schumacher hadn't decided to stop for an ice cream cone on his way home from the police station and that little spider hadn't decided to cross the windshield of the other car and distract the driver, the two cars would not have been in proximity of each other and the accident wouldn't have happened. But it did. Three years later, on his 16th birthday, David, the son of Officer Schumacher, announces to his mother and to the school counselor that he has decided to officially change his name to Blue Avenger, the name of the comic book character he had begun to draw right after his father's death. David—oops, Blue Avenger—goes to school in his father's blue fishing vest and a blue towel tied on his head to begin his new life as the defender of the underdog. Do you think his new look will be noticed?

Curriculum Connection: Psychology

Students deal with peer pressure on a daily basis in high school. Have students discuss Blue Avenger's unusual attire and how he would be treated if he showed up in their school hallway dressed in this manner.

64 Howe, Norma, *Blue Avenger Cracks the Code.*

Holt, 2000, 296pp. $17. ISBN: 0-8050-6372-2
Subjects: Authorship, High Schools
Genres: Humor, Mystery, Realistic
List: Author's Choice
Levels: SLJ 7 & Up, VOYA 7–12

Annotation: Sixteen-year-old David, known as Blue Avenger, first helps his girlfriend find her father and then visits Venice, trying to solve the mystery of who wrote the plays and sonnets attributed to Shakespeare. Companion novel to *The Adventures of Blue Avenger* (Holt, 1999).

Booktalk: Blue Avenger figured out the mystery of why the absent father of his girlfriend, Omaha Brown, visits Rome every year to see Giordano Bruno. It didn't seem possible since Bruno, a 16th century philosopher and heretic, had been burned at the stake by the Inquisition in the year 1600. But while reading a travel guide to Rome, Blue found a reference to the gathering of Giordano Bruno followers at the foot of his statue each year. Blue knew how important it was to Omaha to see and talk to her father, so he had to figure out how to get her to Rome in three days' time. She had to be at the base of Bruno's statue on February 17th, exactly when her father would be there. Why was David, or I should say Blue Avenger, doing this? Well, that's because he was the defender of the underdog and besides, Omaha was his girlfriend. The story doesn't end there. Blue goes to Rome too, and while he is there he sets out to solve an age-old mystery of authorship.

Curriculum Connection: English

The English teacher in this book intrigues Blue with the idea that William Shakespeare did not write the sonnets and plays attributed to him. The author's note discusses Charlton Ogburn's book *The Mysterious William Shakespeare: The Myth and the Reality* (EMP Publications, 1984) and his theory that Edward de Vere, the 17th Earl of Oxford, actually wrote these works. Have students research the controversy concerning Shakespeare's author authenticity.

Hurwin, Davida Wills, *A Time for Dancing.*

65

Little Brown, 1995, 257pp. $15.95. ISBN: 0-316-38351-1. Viking Penguin, 1997, 272pp. $5.99. ISBN: 0-14-038618-1

Subjects: Cancer, Dancing, Death, Friendship
Genre: Realistic
Lists: 2000 B of BBYA, 1997 YAC, 1996 BBYA
Levels: BL 7–12, SLJ 7–10

Annotation: Seventeen-year-olds Samantha and Juliana alternately narrate their feelings about Juliana's diagnosis of cancer and how it will affect their future plans of dancing and college. Juliana goes through therapy but eventually requests to return home to die.

Booktalk: Did you ever wonder how the world continues to revolve even though you are in a crisis situation and you think everything should stop? That's what I thought when Dr. Conner told me that I had cancer. I thought that the nurses should have paused working, traffic in the street should have stopped, and even mothers pushing babies in their strollers should have stopped. How could life go on as usual when I was just told that I have cancer? But life did go on. Even Dr. Conner didn't pause. She just dropped the bomb on me, nodded, and left. And somehow life, at least for now, is going on. I think I am doing better than my best friend, Sam. I can tell when I look at her that she is thinking the same thing I am. I am too young to die. What about all the plans we had made? Our plans to go to college and take dance classes together may never come true, but we have no choice right now but get on with life. I am not dead yet.

Curriculum Connection: Health

Teenagers are not immune to deadly diseases such as cancer. Have students do research on terminally ill teenagers and how they have dealt with their last years or months of life.

66 Huth, Angela, *Land Girls.*

St. Martin's, 1996, 378pp. $23.95. ISBN: 0-312-14296-X. St. Martin's, 1998, 378pp. $12.95. ISBN: 0-312-17195-1
Subjects: Friendship, Relationships, War, World War II
Genre: Historical
List: 2002 PP, 1997 BBYA
Level: Adult

Annotation: Three young women—Agatha, a quiet student; Stella, a young woman in love with a British Naval officer; and Prue, a flirtatious hairdresser—join the war effort and work on a rural English farm during World War II. The farmer's asthmatic son adds a romantic element to the story.

Booktalk: What a young woman wouldn't do to support the war effort in England during World War II! Agatha, Stella, and Prue volunteer to work on a rural farm since the young men are off fighting the war. But not *all* the young men are off to the war. What the three young women don't know is that the farmer's asthmatic son is still on the farm. As soon as Prue sees him, she is intent on romancing him, along with every soldier she can find. Prue is going to do her part to support the war effort! But the farmer's son will fall in love with one of the other "Land Girls."

Curriculum Connection: History

During World War II women in the United States worked in the aircraft factories to help the war effort. In England women also took on roles previously filled by men, working on farms. Have students research the role of women during World War II and how their role varied from one country to another.

67 Jordan, Sherryl, *The Raging Quiet.*

Simon & Schuster, 1999, 266pp. $17. ISBN: 0-689-82140-9. Simon & Schuster, 2000, 272pp. $8. ISBN: 0-689-82877-2
Subjects: Physically Handicapped, Relationships, Witchcraft
Genres: Historical, Romance
List: 2000 BBYA
Levels: BL 8–12, SLJ 8 & Up, VOYA 7–12

Annotation: During the Middle Ages, 16-year-old Marnie is accused of cursing her husband to death, and of witchcraft when she teaches the village madman to use sign language to communicate.

Booktalk: Father Brannan told Marnie she had to pick up the red-hot iron bar firmly across her palm, not just with her fingers. He warned her that she must not drop it, or the ordeal to prove her innocence of witchcraft would start all over again. Marnie's breath came in raspy gasps as she tried to prepare herself for what she knew was coming. Sweat ran in her eyes, and her stomach hurt so much she was sure she was going to be sick. Breathing hard, she faced the glowing iron bar. The witnesses, even her friend the priest, seemed to disappear for Marnie as she concentrated on placing her hand on the red-hot bar. Clamping her lips closed so she would not scream, Marnie wrapped her hand around the bar. The pain exploded up her arm, but she clenched her teeth and took the first of the required nine steps, holding the bar firmly with the palm of her hand.

Curriculum Connection: History

In the past, deaf people were thought to be possessed by demons, as was the case with Raven. Marnie teaches him a form of sign language so he can communicate with her. Have students research the history and development of sign language, including American Sign Language.

Jordan, Sherryl, *Secret Sacrament.*

HarperCollins, 2000, 338pp. $15.95. ISBN: 0-06-028904-X
Subjects: Fathers and Sons, Magic, Occupations, Race Relations, Relationships
Genres: Fantasy, Multicultural, Romance
List: 2002 BBYA
Levels: BL 8–12, SLJ 7 & Up

68

Annotation: The young Navoran healer, Gabriel, goes against the wishes of his father and the Empress in his need to follow his craft and to save the dwindling Shanali nation, which lives just outside the boundaries of the crumbling and corrupt empire.

Booktalk: It was long ago when it happened, but Gabriel could close his eyes and still see her broken and bloodied body lying next to the river. She had heard his footsteps and turned to him with beautiful black eyes, filled with fear. When the native woman saw he was but a child, she pleaded with him to help her. Gabriel was too frightened to help and began to back away, stumbling through the mud at the edge of the river. Something white gleamed in the murky water, and the young boy picked it up. It was a carving strung on a strip of leather. When Gabriel picked it up, the Shanali woman tried to reach up and take it from him, frantically crying out in her native tongue. Seven-year-old Gabriel was so frightened that he ran, with the carving tightly grasped in his fist. Now a young man, he remembered all too well how he had left the woman to die on the river bank, after stealing the only thing that truly mattered to her. Gabriel, now a Healer-in-training at the Citadel, wore the carving around his neck to remind him of the woman and his shame at not helping her. Little did he know that the carving foretold of an ancient prophecy describing the downfall of the Navoran Empire, a downfall in which Gabriel would play a central part.

69 Kerr, M. E., *Deliver Us from Evie.*

Harper Trophy, 1995, 192pp. $4.95. ISBN: 0-06-447128-4
Subjects: Brothers and Sisters, Homosexuality, Occupations
Genre: Realistic
List: 1997 PP
Levels: BL 7–12, SLJ 9 & Up

Annotation: Sixteen-year-old Missouri farm boy Parr and his conservative parents have difficulty accepting his masculine-looking sister, Evie, as a lesbian who is in love with the local banker's daughter.

Booktalk: It was Halloween night, and as usual, the Duffs had invited all the local farmers to their farm. Not that Mr. Duff was really a farmer—he drove a brand-new sports car instead of a tractor. Parr could hear his mother and sister arguing again. His mother was telling Evie that the skirt would fit her just fine, but Evie was refusing to wear it. His mother came down the stairs looking beautiful in a black skirt and blouse. Evie came down in jeans, boots, and a T-shirt that read GET HIGH ON MILK! OUR COWS ARE ON GRASS! Whereas his mother's long, blonde hair streamed down her back, Evie wore her dark hair very short with a streak of blond in the front. Parr realized that rather than looking like their petite blonde mother, Evie looked like Elvis. He knew that night, as he looked at his mother and sister, that Evie would never be a typical Missouri farm girl. But what Parr did not know was that Evie was about to begin a relationship that night—at the Duff's Halloween party—that would tear his family apart.

Curriculum Connection: Career Education

Parr does not want to follow in his father's footsteps and become a farmer. He wants to go away to college and begin a different type of career, away from the family farm. He and his older brother think that they are "off the hook" in relation to the farm because their sister is the one who loves to be out in the fields with their father. But when Evie gets involved in a relationship and leaves home, Parr fears he will be the one expected to stay on the farm. Have students discuss family expectations in reference to family businesses.

70

Kerr, M. E., *"Hello, I Lied."*

HarperCollins, 1997, 171pp. $15.95. ISBN: 0-06-027529-4. HarperTrophy, 1998, 171pp. $4.95. ISBN: 0-06-447193-4

Subjects: Friendship, Homosexuality, Music, Sexual Relationships
Genre: Realistic
List: Author's Choice
Levels: BL 9–12, SLJ 10 & Up

Annotation: Seventeen-year-old Lang spends the summer in the Hamptons with his mother, who is working for a reclusive and aging rock star. Lang resents leaving behind his boyfriend in New York City and questions his sexuality when he becomes infatuated with a girl from France.

Booktalk: Lang hardly ever saw Ben Nevada, the reclusive rock star his mother worked for. So why was he getting an invitation from Nevada to have lunch with him? It didn't take long before Lang figured out what Nevada wanted. Friends of Nevada's who lived in France had a 17-year-old daughter who had fallen in love with a peasant, a grape picker, of all things. Her parents wanted to put an end to this romance so they were sending her to live with Nevada for the summer. And Nevada wanted Lang to entertain her while she was there. Nevada thought a gay guy entertaining her was a great idea, no worries about any romantic involvement. If he had only known what would happen between Lang and Hugette during the course of her visit, Nevada would never have asked Lang to spend time with her.

71

Klass, David, *California Blue.*

Scholastic, 1994, 224pp. $13.95. ISBN: 0-590-46688-7. Scholastic, 1996, 199pp. $3.99. ISBN: 0-590-46689-5

Subjects: Cancer, Ecology, Fathers and Sons, Track and Field
Genres: Realistic, Sports
Lists: 1998 PP, 1996 YAC
Levels: BL 7–10, SLJ 8–12

Annotation: While running among the California redwoods, 17-year-old John discovers a species of butterfly that exists nowhere else in the world. Reporting its existence to the scientists at the university makes him an outcast in his small lumber-mill town.

Booktalk: Mom was talking too much over dinner. When she started to cry and ran out of the room, I got up to go after her. Dad told me to sit back down. It wasn't quite an order, but close. He's looking up from his plate and we're studying each other. We don't get along very well, and I'm wondering what he wants. I had decided a long time ago that, since everyone says what a great father he is, the problem must be me. I admit that there were lots of time when he tried to push me one way that I automatically went the other. I honestly don't know why, because my brothers and sisters didn't. They all seem to be living perfect lives with families of their own. I am the unlucky one still living at home, and I know he is about to tell me something I don't want to know.

Curriculum Connection: Science

John finds a species of butterfly that exists nowhere else in the world. Have students do research on species that are indigenous to only one area of the world. What are the citizens of the country in which the species lives doing to protect it from extinction?

72 Klass, David, *Danger Zone.*

Scholastic, 1996, 232pp. $16.95. ISBN: 0-590-48590-3. Scholastic, 1998, 240pp. $4.50. ISBN: 0-590-48591-1
Subjects: African Americans, Basketball, Race Relations
Genres: Multicultural, Sports
Lists: 1999 PP, 1998 YAC, 1997 BBYA
Levels: BL 7–12, SLJ 7–10

Annotation: When Minnesotan high school junior Jimmy Doyle joins the predominantly African-American High School Dream Team basketball team, he learns about racial prejudice both on and off the court and while in Rome, Italy.

Booktalk: Jimmy couldn't believe he was leaving his small town in Minnesota to play a starting position on the American "Dream Team." But being on this team was no sweet dream. They hadn't even left for Rome yet and he was tired of dealing with Augustus LeMay, the black player who Jimmy was sure hated him because he was white, but even more so because he took LeMay's friend's spot on the team. If Jimmy was going to survive this experience, he was going to have to learn how to deal with LeMay, both on and off the court.

Curriculum Connections: Physical Education, Psychology

Jimmy is an all-American white guy from Minnesota. Have students discuss whether it is possible for him to be experiencing racial prejudice as a white guy on a basketball team full of black guys. Do you have to be a member of a minority group to experience prejudice?

73

Klass, David, *Screen Test.*
Scholastic, 1997, 251pp. $16.95. ISBN: 0-590-48592-X
Subjects: Occupations, Relationships
Genres: Realistic, Romance
List: 1999 YAC
Levels: BL 7–9, SLJ 7–10

Annotation: Sixteen-year-old Liz is starring in a movie with one of Hollywood's most handsome young actors. The glamorous lifestyle, the money, and an attraction to her costar are making her rethink her future and her plans to go to college. The rose-colored glasses come off when Liz discovers that this older-than-he-said-he-was costar had been lying to her.

Booktalk: Why would anyone turn down the chance to be a movie star living a life of luxury in Hollywood? That is the very question 16-year-old Liz is asking herself. Who knew that a bit part in a neighbor's feature film would land her a part in a real movie working with Tommy Fletcher, one of the most eligible hunks in Hollywood? Liz can't help but be pulled into Tommy's glamorous lifestyle, but is he telling her the truth about himself?

Curriculum Connection: Career Education
    Liz initially is excited about working in the movie industry as an actress. But the longer she stays in Hollywood, the less enamored she is with the lifestyle of the movie stars. Have students do research on teen actors and actresses, and how their acting experience affects their lives.

74

Klause, Annette Curtis, *Blood and Chocolate.*
Delacorte, 1997, 264pp. $16.95. ISBN 0-385-32305-0. Dell, 1999, 288pp. $4.99. ISBN: 0-440-22668-6
Subjects: Relationships, Werewolves
Genres: Horror, Romance
Lists: 2000 PP, 1999 YAC, 1998 BBYA, 1998 QP
Levels: BL 11 & Up, SLJ 9 & Up, VOYA 10–12

Annotation: Vivian is a teenage werewolf trying to come to terms with her animal versus human feelings after she falls in love with a human boy. When she shows her true self to her human boyfriend, he is terrified, and her disclosure endangers her pack.

Booktalk: Much to her dismay, Vivian has fallen for a "meat-boy." She wants to bite the buttons right off of his shirt—an appropriate response for a werewolf! Vivian knows it is best to stick to her own kind, but she finds Aiden's human sensitivity and gentleness so attractive. On the other hand, Vivian is proud of her sleek and sensual werewolf side. She wants to share all of who, and what, she is with Aiden. But when she transforms right before his very eyes, her "meat-boy" isn't enchanted by her sleek wolf body as she had expected; he is terrified of her. In her desperate attempt to win Aiden's love, Vivian has put her pack in danger.

75 Klause, Annette Curtis, *The Silver Kiss.*

Bantam Doubleday Dell, 1992, 198pp. $3.99. ISBN: 0-440-21346-0
Subjects: Brothers, Cancer, Death, Relationships, Vampires
Genres: Horror, Romance, Supernatural
Lists: 1994 B of BBYA, 2000 B of BBYA, 1999 PP
Level: BL 8–12

Annotation: Zoe, who feels frightened and alone because her mother is in the hospital dying of cancer, becomes infatuated with a vampire she meets in the park. She helps him avenge the death of his mother by killing his little brother, who also is a vampire.

Booktalk: When Simon saw her for the first time in the park, he ran away, wiping the rat's blood from his mouth. The second time he saw her in the park, she ran away from him, angry that he was on her park bench. This time he followed her home and watched her through the window. He couldn't go in unless he was invited, but he checked the doors and windows so he knew how he could get in when it was time. The animal was close to the surface tonight. He remembered the time, right after he changed, when he savagely tore the neck open on the gamekeeper. He was out of the forest now, but the forest would always be a part of him. He marked his territory like a wolf, by urinating on the door. She would be his. Simon was sure of that.

Curriculum Connection: English

Have students read a modern vampire novel, such as *The Silver Kiss*, and then read *Dracula* by Bram Stoker, comparing the myth and lore surrounding vampires and how the myths are similar or different between the two books.

76

Krisher, Trudy, *Kinship.*

Delacorte, 1997, 304pp. $15.95. ISBN: 0-385-32272-0. Bantam Doubleday Dell, 1999, 304pp. $4.50. ISBN: 0-440-22023-8

Subjects: Brothers and Sisters, Family Problems, Fathers and Daughters, Mothers and Daughters
Genre: Realistic
List: 1998 BBYA
Levels: BL 7–10, SLJ 6–10, VOYA 6–9

Annotation: When the long-absent father of 15-year-old Pert returns to their small Georgia town of Kinship, Pert learns the difference between kin and family, with the help of her brother and their trailer park neighbors. Companion novel to *Spite Fences* (Laurel Leaf, 1996).

Booktalk: When he came home I couldn't understand why Rae Jean (that's what I call my mother) and Jimmy weren't happy. I always wanted to know my Daddy. And when he said he would take me to the Hayes County High School Father-Daughter Dance, I was so excited and proud to be able to walk into the dance with him. He was supposed to meet me there, but he never showed up. My big brother Jimmy did. He even brought me flowers. As my big brother danced me around the floor, I remembered Ida Weevil telling me that there was a big difference between family and kin. Daddy will always be family, but that night I realized that he does not belong with us in Kinship.

Curriculum Connection: Psychology
   Have students discuss whether you have to be related by blood to be family or kin. In this day of blended family situations, how does one define family? What does Pert mean by "kin"?

77

Lane, Dakota, *Johnny Voodoo.*

Bantam Doubleday Dell, 1997, 208pp. $4.50. ISBN: 0-440-21998-1

Subjects: Death, Family Problems, Fathers and Daughters, High Schools, Moving, Music, Race Relations, Relationships
Genres: Multicultural, Realistic, Romance
Lists: 2000 PP, 1998 YAC, 1997 BBYA
Levels: BL 9–12, SLJ 8–12

Annotation: Fifteen-year-old Deidre is grieving the death of her mother and her way of life in Manhattan when her father moves them to a small town in Louisiana. Here she meets a strange young man who shows her the bayous and how to love again.

Booktalk: Deidre didn't care what they said about Johnny at school. She didn't care that they made fun of him living in the swamps and called him Johnny Voodoo. All she cared about was how he made her feel. And when he said he loved her, that she was his other half, Deidre felt whole. It was the first time she hadn't felt alone since her mom died. During her time with Johnny, Deidre also had realized something about relationships and love. Before she met Johnny, she had hated all the terms for sex, including making love. But as she lay on the grass with Johnny, fully clothed, watching the stars, she knew, as he kissed her and touched her face, that they were truly making love. She knew loving someone had little to do with the act of sex; it had to do with intimacy, caring, and understanding.

78. Lee, Marie G., *Necessary Roughness.*

HarperCollins, 1996, 240pp. $14.95. ISBN: 0-06-025124-7. HarperCollins, 1998, 228pp. $4.95. ISBN: 0-06-447169-1
Subjects: Fathers and Sons, Football, Korean Americans, Moving, Race Relations
Genres: Multicultural, Realistic, Sports
List: 1998 BBYA
Levels: BL 7–12, SLJ 7–10

Annotation: Sixteen-year-old Chan's Korean family moves to rural Minnesota, where he experiences prejudice on and off of the football field. Chan also is dealing with his domineering father.

Booktalk: In hindsight maybe I shouldn't have suggested we leave the Buddha behind, but we are Christian after all. We even say grace before meals. It wasn't like I suggested we leave my sister behind. But Abogee ("father" in Korean) was furious with my comment. He doesn't blow up and shout when he's mad at me, instead, he refuses to speak to or look at me. He did just that—with O-Ma ("mother") in the front seat, my twin sister, Young, and me in the back seat, and that ugly, gold-painted, stone Buddha weighing down the back of our beat-up station wagon—all the way to Minnesota. Considering the circumstances, I decided not to ask him why we were moving from L.A. to Minnesota, land of ten thousand hicks.

Curriculum Connections: Math, Sociology

Prejudice and ignorance go hand in hand. Have students surveys their peers in relation to their ethnic background. Students then compare the numbers of each ethnic group, creating visual charts to show the percentage of each group.

Lester, Julius, *Othello: A Novel.*

Scholastic, 1995, 151pp. $14.95. ISBN: 0-590-41967-6. Scholastic, 1998, 151pp. $3.99. ISBN: 0-590-41966-8.
Subjects: Death, Friendship, Murder, Race Relations, Relationships
Genres: Historical, Multicultural, Romance
List: 1996 BBYA
Levels: BL 8–12, SLJ 8 & Up

Annotation: This is a retelling of Shakespeare's *Othello* set in England, with Othello, Iago, and Emilia coming from Africa. The powerful black general, Othello, believes his friend Iago when he lies and says that his young white wife, Desdemona, has been unfaithful, and Othello kills her.

Booktalk: Intrigue and love are typically present in any Shakespeare play, but reading the play format can make the story a bit difficult to understand. Lester has taken the story of Othello and his beautiful young wife, Desdemona, and has made it much easier to read by writing it as a novel. Most of you know the story of Romeo and Juliet and how Romeo commits suicide when he finds Juliet dead. The story of Othello also is a love story with a tragic death, but it differs quite a bit in that the main character, Othello, is a black general who marries a young, noble, white English woman. Desdemona adores her husband, but Othello's best friend becomes jealous and is intent on breaking them up. From here the story of Othello and Desdemona takes a different path, but is as tragic as the one of Romeo and Juliet.

Curriculum Connection: English

Julius Lester has taken liberties with the Shakespearean tale of Othello. He changed the setting to England and changed the characters of Iago and Emily (Emilia) to Africans. But the rest of the retelling stays true. Lester has merged modernized dialogue from the play into his retelling. Have students compare the modernized dialogue with the original play to help them understand what the original dialogue means.

80 Levenkron, Steven, *The Luckiest Girl in the World.*

Viking Penguin, 1998, 192pp. $9.95. ISBN 0-140-26625-9
Subjects: Emotional Problems, Figure Skating, Mental Illness, Mothers and Daughters
Genres: Realistic, Sports
List: 1998 BBYA
Level: Adult

Annotation: Fifteen-year-old Katie, a private school student on a scholarship, cuts her arms until they bleed with a pair of small sewing scissors when she can't handle the stress of school and trying to be the figure skater her mother wants her to be.

Booktalk: Katie takes out the pair of sewing scissors she hides just for this purpose. She digs them into the inside fleshy part of her arm until she breaks the skin, drawing blood, causing physical pain, to distract herself from the much deeper pain of knowing she will never be the talented figure skater her mother expects her to be. Katie feels like she has the weight of the world on her shoulders, but from the outside looking in, Katie appears to be the luckiest girl in the world. Appearances can be quite deceiving.

Curriculum Connections: Health, Psychology
Self-mutilation is a way of easing emotional pain by focusing on the physical pain. Have students discuss healthy ways a person can diffuse an anxiety attack or other type of emotional pain.

81 Levitin, Sonia, *The Cure.*

Harcourt, 1999, 180pp. $16. ISBN: 0-15-201827-1. HarperTrophy, 2000, 260pp. $4.95. ISBN: 0-380-73298-X
Subjects: Death, Epidemics, Jews, Middle Ages, Music, Race Relations, Time Travel
Genres: Historical, Multicultural, Science Fiction
List: Author's Choice
Levels: BL 6–9, SLJ 7–10, VOYA 6–9

Annotation: In a dystopian society, during the year 2407, a 16-year-old boy is punished for his nonconformity by being sent to the Middle Ages, a time when villagers who feared that the Jews were the cause of the Black Plague burned them to death.

Booktalk: Gemm 16884 has been deemed a deviant in the Utopian society of Conformity, Harmony, and Tranquility in the year 2407. His deviant behavior involves his response to music and his desire to dance and sing, both of which are not allowed in this society. The Elders give him two options—to be recycled or to go through the Cure. They tell him to choose wisely, as the Cure will be quite painful. The Elders had already looked into the files "From Past Time" and had found an event in history that they are sure will cure him of his deviant desire to make music. If Gemm 16884 had known what he was in for during the Cure, he may have chosen to be recycled.

83 Lynch, Chris, *Extreme Elvin.*

HarperCollins, 1999, 230pp. $15.89. ISBN: 0-06-028210-X. HarperCollins, 2001, 240pp. $5.95. ISBN: 0-06-447142-X
Subjects: Friendship, High Schools, Mothers and Sons, Relationships, Weight Control
Genres: Humor, Realistic
List: Author's Choice
Levels: K 7–10, SLJ 8–10

Annotation: Fourteen-year-old Elvin enters high school, finds a girlfriend, and learns to deal with the mistreatment an overweight freshman experiences, with the help of his friends Mikie and Frankie. Companion novel to *Slot Machine* (HarperCollins, 1995).

Booktalk: I had my first experience with a girl at the Catholic girls' school freshman dance. This really good-looking girl actually touched me. Mikie asked me if it itched where she touched me, and I scratched the top of my hand, hoping to feel some sensation, but nothing as of yet. I was a bit worried that by Monday all the guys would forget about it. I told Mikie I needed evidence of my triumph. Mikie looked at me like I was nuts and told me that most people would see getting scabies as a negative experience, not a triumph. Then he asked me if I knew what scabies was. Well, I thought I did, but I really didn't and tried to bluff my way out of it by saying it was like an allergy or hives—it made you itch. When Mikie told me that scabies was caused by bugs, I thought he was joking. Then he proceeded to tell me that these creepy little insects actually went under your skin and laid eggs there. They had babies inside you! The babies made tunnels inside you. I had thought they were cute little things, not gross bugs. Like I wasn't freaked out enough before he told me that they could spread to other parts of my body. I didn't start hyperventilating until he asked me if my hand had been socializing with any other parts of my body. Oh my God!!

Curriculum Connection: Health

Elvin is quite overweight and tries to diet to lose weight. Have students research the different types of diets that have been popular through the years, such as the grapefruit diet, the no fat diet, and so on. For their research, have them determine whether they think fad diets are a healthy or effective way to lose weight.

Curriculum Connection: History

The historical portion of this novel is based on fact. On February 14, 1349, the Jews of Strasbourg were burned to death because of false accusations that they had poisoned the water wells, causing the Black Plague. Racial prejudice is certainly not a modern-day occurrence. Have students research race relations during the Middle Ages. Levitin includes a short bibliography to assist students in beginning their research.

Logue, Mary, *Dancing with an Alien.*

HarperCollins, 2000, 134pp. $14.89. ISBN: 0-06-028319-X. HarperCollins, 2002, 144pp. $6.95. ISBN: 0-06-447209-4
Subjects: Extraterrestrial Beings, Friendship, Medical Experimentation, Pregnancy, Relationships, Swimming
Genres: Romance, Science Fiction
Lists: 2001 BBYA, 2001 QP
Levels: SLJ 8–10, VOYA 7–12

Annotation: Seventeen-year-old Tonia and the alien Branko narrate the development of their relationship when he arrives in Minnesota intent on bringing back to his planet a human female to bear multiple children.

Booktalk: It hadn't crossed Tonia's mind that her very tall boyfriend might be an alien from another planet, rather than an exchange student from Romania. He did talk funny and walked out into the lake until his head was under water rather than swimming, but she thought he was just different. Of course it was her best friend, Beatrice, who brought it up; after all, she was the one who believed in life on other planets. Tonia was an agnostic in relation to extraterrestrials, but when she fell in love with Branko, she started to wonder about his lack of relationship skills and really needed to know who, or what, he was. He kept saying that he had to go home soon and she didn't want to lose him, but where exactly was his home? Beatrice kept bugging Tonia to ask him where he really was from and when she did, Branko admitted he was an alien. Tonia was in shock. Part of her just would not believe him—that is, not until he opened his shirt and pulled his nipples off. Then she believed!

Curriculum Connection: English

This book is considered science fiction rather than fantasy because there is nothing in this book that could not take place in the future, or even today. There is no magic involved in the arrival of Branko on Earth—a ship brought him here. Have students discuss the other "unusual" things that happen in this book and how feasible they are in the world as we know it.

Lynch, Chris, *Iceman.*

HarperCollins, 1994, $15. ISBN: 0-06-23340-0. HarperTrophy, 1995, 181pp. $3.95. ISBN: 0-06-447114-4
Subjects: Brothers, Hockey, Parent and Child
Genres: Realistic, Sports
List: 1999 PP
Levels: BL 8–12, SLJ–10

Annotation: Fourteen-year-old Eric, a ruthless hockey player, takes out his anger toward his hockey-addicted father and overly religious mother on the rink. When he isn't playing hockey, Eric hangs out in the local mortuary.

Booktalk: I'm not a great hockey player like my brother, but I always lead my team in points. It's not because I am such a great hockey player; it's because of the way I play. I play hard. It isn't skill that gets me the shot; I either intimidate the guy into giving the puck to me, or I ram him, along with the puck, into the net. They call me the Iceman because I am heartless. Coach says I'd skate over the top of my own mother to get to the puck. What they don't know about is the burning inside of me. How can I be both fire and ice?

Curriculum Connection: Physical Education
Have students discuss why athletes aren't thought of as smart, but as "dumb jocks," even though it takes strategic planning to play sports. Is anger necessary to play an aggressive sport such as hockey or football?

Lynch, Chris, *Slot Machine.*

HarperCollins, 1995, 241pp. $14.95. ISBN: 0-06-023584-5. HarperTrophy, 1996, 256pp. $5.95. ISBN: 0-06-447140-3
Subjects: Friendship, Letter Writing, Mothers and Sons, Weight Control, Wrestling
Genres: Humor, Sports
Lists: 1997 YAC, 1996 BBYA, 1996 QP
Levels: BL 8–10, SLJ 7–10

Annotation: Elvin and his two friends, Frankie and Mikie, attend summer camp to determine what sport slot they will fit into in their new, all-male Catholic high school. Overweight Elvin discovers, after trying several sports, such as football and wrestling, that his slot for the time being is to watch. Companion novel to *Extreme Elvin* (HarperCollins, 1999).

Booktalk: Being a fat kid in school was not easy, but Elvin made the best of it, using his sense of humor whenever he could. Elvin's attitude was: Why not make fun of yourself before anyone else could? Summer camp for his new high school had barely begun and Elvin had already thrown up baked beans through his nose when they tried to slot him as a football player, and he woke up in the middle of the night with his bed in a frog-infested pond. But neither of those was his most embarrassing moment at summer camp. The most embarrassing was when his mom got a beer out of the ice-filled trashcans during family weekend. The other mothers were drinking iced tea like ladies, with their little pinkies up in the air, but not his mother. Elvin tried to be a good sport about it until one of the football players called out, "That's Elvin's father." That's when he got his mother out of there.

Curriculum Connection: Physical Education

Have students discuss the personality traits of sports lovers vs. non-sports lovers. What if a guy doesn't like, or isn't good at, sports? How will this disinterest or dislike of sports affect a guy's treatment in school?

86 Lynch, Chris, **Whitechurch.**

HarperCollins, 1999, 247pp. $14.89. ISBN: 0-06-28331-9. HarperTrophy, 2000, 256pp. $7.95. ISBN: 0-06-447143-8
Subjects: Death, Friendship, Mental Illness, Murder
Genre: Realistic
List: Author's Choice
Level: SLJ 9 & Up

Annotation: The breakdown of the relationship among three teens, one of them mentally unstable, occurs because both boys are in love with the girl. Jealousy results in the murder of an innocent visitor to their small town.

Booktalk: Oakley and Pauly had been friends for years. Oakley knew that Pauly was more than a bit off the wall at times. Everyone in town thought he was crazy, but that didn't stop Oakley from being his best friend. Even when Pauly scared Lilly away with his antics with the gun, Oakley still stayed, assuring his friend that he wasn't leaving too. He sat down on the ground next to Pauly. All of a sudden Pauly put the barrel of the Colt .45 semiautomatic in his own mouth. The gun was so big it barely fit, but Pauly grinned at Oakley around the barrel. Oakley thought he was going to lose it, and his face turned green. Pauly was thoroughly pleased with his friend's reaction. But that wasn't enough for Pauly. He needed a bigger adrenalin rush and put the barrel up against Oakley's lips and told his best friend to put it in his mouth.

Marchetta, Melina, *Looking for Alibrandi.*

Orchard, 1999, 250pp. $17.99. ISBN: 0-531-33142-3
Subjects: Fathers and Daughters, High Schools, Mothers and Daughters, Pregnancy, Relationships
Genres: Multicultural, Realistic
List: 2000 BBYA
Levels: BL 8–10, SLJ 9–12

Annotation: Seventeen-year-old Josie, from a close Italian family, is a scholarship student at a private Catholic school in Sydney, Australia. After years of dealing with ethnic slurs and rude comments about her illegitimacy, Josie's life changes when her father returns and she begins to date an Aussie.

Booktalk: The Aussies at school call Josie an ethnic, or a wog, because she is Italian. And her own people call her worse because her mother didn't marry her father. Her grandmother and mother are always telling her what she can and cannot do in relation to how it will reflect on her family. Then Josie meets and falls in love with Jacob, an Aussie, who doesn't understand why she can't just live her life the way she wants. He doesn't understand that her culture is so much a part of her that there is no escape. And now with her Italian father back in her life, Josie isn't so sure that she wants to escape her culture.

Curriculum Connections: History, Sociology

In the United States, we often think of black vs. white in relation to prejudices. However, ethnic prejudice can be colorblind. Josie is an Italian-Australian, an ethnic minority in that country, and is treated as such. Ethnic prejudice also is evident in the United States. Have students research how the early Irish immigrants and other ethnic groups were treated when they first came to the United States.

88 Marsden, John, *Tomorrow When the War Began.*

(The Tomorrow series, #1) Houghton Mifflin, 1995, 288pp. $15. ISBN: 0-395-70673-4. Bantam Doubleday Dell, 1996, 286pp. $3.99.
ISBN: 0-440-21985-X
Subjects: Camping, Friendship, Survival, War
Genre: Adventure
Lists: 2000 B of BBYA, 1998 PP, 1996 BBYA
Levels: BL 9–12, SLJ 8 & Up

Annotation: Six Australian teenagers return from a camping trip to a remote area of Australia to find their town has been invaded and their families are prisoners. The teens must work together to free their families. Book 1 of the *Tomorrow* series.

Booktalk: Imagine that you and six of your friends decide to go camping in a remote area. You are so remote that your cell phones don't work, and you have no contact with your family until you return. But while you were out exploring the wilderness, your hometown has been invaded, not by some scary science-fiction-type monsters from outer space, like in the movies, but by real men, carrying real weapons, and you don't know where your families are. Would you sit back and wait for them to take you too, or would you be like the friends in *Tomorrow When the War Began* and fight back?

Curriculum Connection: History
   A world war has never begun in the United States, or in Australia for that matter, as is the setting for this book. However, both the United States and Australia fought in both World Wars I and II. The United States was a major world power then and still is today. Australia is not considered a major world power. Have students discuss why they think Australia got involved in both world wars.

89 Martinez, Victor, *Parrot in the Oven.*

HarperCollins, 1996, 225pp. $15.89. ISBN: 0-06-026-706-2. HarperTrophy, 1998, 216pp. $5.95. ISBN: 0-06-447186-1
Subjects: Alcoholism, Family Problems, Gangs, Mexican Americans
Genres: Multicultural, Realistic
List: Author's Choice
Award: Pura Belpre
Levels: BL 7–10, SLJ 8–10

Annotation: Fourteen-year-old Manny is trying to find his place in the world by joining a gang, while his family is in turmoil because of his father's alcoholism, his sister's pregnancy, and his lazy brother's behavior.

Booktalk: Manny's mom knew, when day two rolled around and his dad hadn't come home yet, that it was time to go get him from the pool hall. When they walked through the door, his dad's friends rolled their eyes, and the owner said he had gone home. But Manny's mom was too smart for that. She found him hiding in one of the bathroom stalls, but he refused to come home. Manny's mom knew the look on his face and headed home, fearfully looking behind her to see if he was following. She sent his sister to a friend's house and headed to the beauty parlor, leaving Manny alone to face his irate father. Manny knew it was going to be even worse than he thought when his father said he would fix her when he found her, while he pulled his old rifle down from the top of the bedroom closet.

Mazer, Norma Fox, *Out of Control.*

90

Morrow, 1993, 224pp. $16. ISBN: 0-688-10208-5. Morrow, 1994, 218pp. $4.99. ISBN: 0-380-71347-0
Subjects: High Schools, Sexual Assault
Genre: Realistic
List: Author's Choice
Level: BL 9–12

Annotation: A 14-year-old girl leaves a high school assembly and is sexually assaulted by three boys, but when she reports it to the school authorities they only want to cover it up. Only one of the boys feels any remorse for his behavior.

Booktalk: Valerie was walking up to the high school when she saw the three boys sitting on the steps. One of them saw her coming and purposely sprawled out across the step. Valerie asked him to move, but he only asked her why and stayed where he was. So Valerie decided to walk up the stairs anyway. He didn't move and she stepped on his hand with her booted foot. The guy swore and slapped her on the leg, and Valerie jumped like a chicken when he touched her. Perhaps Valerie wouldn't have tried to get past the three guys on the steps if she knew what they would do to her when they found her alone on the third floor of the school.

Curriculum Connections: Health, Psychology

Valerie is assaulted when three boys find her alone in a school hallway. The boys did not rape her; she was mauled through her clothes. Have the students discuss why some of the characters in the story do not see this incident as sexual assault, explaining their opinion of the difference between sexual assault and hallway "horseplay." Students can then discuss the different ways sexual assault can be defined and create their own definition of sexual assault, using library materials as well as their class discussion.

91 Mazer, Norma Fox, *When She Was Good.*

Scholastic, 1997, 228pp. $16.95. ISBN: 0-590-13506-6. Scholastic, 2000, 240pp. $4.99. ISBN: 0-590-31990-6
Subjects: Child Abuse, Emotional Problems, Family Problems, Mental Illness, Sisters
Genre: Realistic
List: 1998 BBYA
Levels: BL 10–12, SLJ 8 & Up, VOYA 10–12

Annotation: After her abusive older sister dies, emotionally unbalanced 17-year-old Mem remembers and has flashbacks of her abusive family situation as she tries to build a life on her own.

Booktalk: I know Pamela is dead, but I keep hearing her angry voice in my head, and it freaks me out. Like when we were living in the shelter after getting thrown out of the apartment because she didn't pay the rent. Mr. Elias was trying to help us. He knew Pamela wasn't right in the head. He was trying to get her a disability check, and she had to go to see the psychiatrists. It really made her mad, and she took it out on me. Her cheeks got all red, and she called the doctor a turd and Mr. Elias a moron, and then she slapped me. But I didn't cry. I never cried when she hit or pinched me. Now I can't seem to stop crying. I have been crying for days on end. I don't understand why now. For all those years that Pamela hit me, I never cried. I was so proud of how brave I was. And now, when Pamela is gone and I don't have to worry about being hit anymore, I can't stop crying. Like I said, I know she is dead, but I still keep hearing her angry voice in my head.

92 McCants, William D., *Much Ado About Prom Night.*

Harcourt Brace, 1995, 192pp. $11. ISBN: 0-15-200083-6. Harcourt Brace, 1995, 232pp. $5. 0-15-200081-X
Subjects: High Schools, Relationships
Genres: Humor, Realistic
Lists: 2000 PP, 1997 YAC, 1996 BBYA, 1996 QP
Level: SLJ 7 & Up

Annotation: Rebecca, head of the high school peer counseling program, and Jeff, editor of the school newspaper, butt heads over high school politics, but eventually discover how much they care about each other.

Booktalk: I cannot believe him! How dare he write a column in the Beacon questioning the need for the Peer Counseling Network and the qualifications of my staff? He thought he had shut us down in February when he questioned the ability of teenagers to keep the secrets of students coming in to us with problems. And now that we are busier than ever, he decides to write another column about us. And that stupid comment about students who are unsuccessful in their quest for prom dates being able to sue the high school for pain and suffering. He's gone too far this time. I am going down to the newspaper room and let him have a piece of my mind. It's high time to verbally kick some butt!

Curriculum Connection: Psychology

Have students discuss whether peer counseling is appropriate in the high school setting. Can peer counselors keep the sessions confidential? When is it appropriate to tell a teacher or other adult about what was disclosed in a peer counseling session?

McDonald, Joyce, *Swallowing Stones.*

93

Delacorte, 1997, 245pp. $15.95. ISBN: 0-385-32309-3. Bantam Doubleday Dell, 1999, 256pp. $4.99. ISBN: 0-440-22672-4

Subjects: Death, Friendship
Genre: Realistic
Lists: 2000 B of BBYA, 1998 BBYA
Levels: BL 7–10, SLJ 7–12, VOYA 7–12

Annotation: Fifteen-year-old Jenna, the daughter of the man who died, and Michael, the 17-year-old who killed him by firing a shot into the air, tell the story of how Jenna deals with her grief and how Michael deals with his guilt over not initially admitting he fired the deadly shot.

Booktalk: Michael tried to bury his guilt, like he did the gun, after he realized it was the single bullet he fired into the air from the rifle he received as a birthday present that killed the man repairing his roof. His guilt became even more intense when he met Jenna, the daughter of the guy he had killed. He could see in her face the pain she was going through, and he wanted to help. The best Michael could do was sit vigil on the church steps across from her house. What he didn't know was that Jenna had been watching him from her bedroom window, counting the evenings he was there, 10 so far, and wondering why he was there and who he was waiting for. She had no idea he was waiting for her.

Curriculum Connection: English

Michael felt like he was "swallowing stones" because of the guilt he felt over the death of Jenna's father. Have students brainstorm other expressions we use to describe how we feel, such as "butterflies in my stomach."

---

94 Meyer, Carolyn, *Drummers of Jericho.*

Harcourt Brace, 1995, 336pp. $11. ISBN: 0-15-200441-6. Harcourt Brace, 1995, 308pp. $5. ISBN: 0-15-200190-5
Subjects: High Schools, Jewish Americans, Music, Race Relations, Stepfamilies
Genres: Multicultural, Realistic
Lists: 1996 BBYA, 1997 PP
Levels: BL 6–9, SLJ 6–10

Annotation: Pazit, a 14-year-old Jewish American, moves from Denver to live with her father and stepmother in the small conservative town of Jericho. She experiences religious prejudice when she objects to the high school band playing hymns at the football games. Billy, a drummer in the school band, loses his standing in the community when he supports Pazit.

Booktalk: Pazit had never felt so out of place in her entire life, not even when she started school in Israel. Within a day she was riding around Tel Aviv with Rachel and had found friends in the dorm. This small Southern town was totally different. She hadn't meant for her dad to call the American Civil Liberties Union when she told him about the hymns being played at the football games. Being out of place was one thing, but now people were getting vicious. As Pazit walked through the hallways of the high school, she heard them calling her a Jew bitch, telling her to get out of their school.

Curriculum Connections: Government, Psychology, Sociology

There is separation of church and state in the United States. Have students research what this means and how it relates to prayer in school, Christmas pageants, and hymns being played at football games.

Moore, Martha, *Angels on the Roof.*

Dell, 1999, 192pp. $4.99. ISBN: 0-440-22806-9
Subjects: Child Abuse, Family Problems, Mothers and Daughters, Moving
Genre: Realistic
List: Author's Choice
Levels: BL 7–9, SLJ 7–10, VOYA 7–12

Annotation: Fourteen-year-old Shelby is frustrated with her mother and her recent decision to move to Texas, where she had been raised by a foster mother. But it is in this small Texas town that Shelby discovers that her father had been abusive, explaining why her mother moved them so often.

Booktalk: Shelby had been asking her mother for years to tell her about her father, but her mother flatly refused. The more secretive she was, the more Shelby wanted to know. When her mother moved them back to Texas, where her mother had lived in a foster home, Shelby realized that this was where her mother and father had met and married. Now she could get to the bottom of why her mother would not talk about him. Shelby continued to dig for clues to her father's whereabouts and eventually found pictures of her parents. The pictures didn't tell Shelby much. Her father's face had been cut out of each one. It wasn't until she went down into the root cellar and found the faces scattered all over the floor that the painful, early childhood memories came rushing back. Shelby then knew why her mother kept moving them from town to town.

Curriculum Connection: Art
   Georgia O'Keefe and her art fascinates Shelby's mother. She even dresses in black like Georgia O'Keefe. Have students research O'Keefe in relation to her different types of art, such as the western, the urban, and her detailed flowers.

Mori, Kyoko, *One Bird.*

Ballantine, 1996, 244pp. $4.50. ISBN: 0-449-70453-X
Subjects: Divorce, Japanese, Mothers and Daughters, Occupations
Genre: Multicultural
List: 1996 BBYA
Levels: BL 8–12, SLJ 7–10

Annotation: In 1970s Japan, 15-year-old Megumi gets a part-time job with a female veterinarian helping take care of sick birds. At the same time, she learns to accept her parents' unconventional divorce and having to live with her undemonstrative father and grandmother.

Booktalk: Divorce is thought of quite differently in Japan than in the United States. When parents divorce, the children typically do not live with their mother. So when Megumi's mother told her daughter she wished she could take her with her, Megumi knew there was no use in wishing—it was not going to happen. Mother had told her many times that if a woman leaves her husband, the children have to stay with their father and the woman must return to live with her own parents for the rest of her life. She would not be allowed to see her own children until they were adults. Megumi knew her mother had told her this many times to prepare her, because if she took Megumi with her, Megumi would grow up in shame, despised by strangers and neighbors as a fatherless child. And now Megumi's greatest fear was coming true—her mother was leaving her father.

Curriculum Connections: Math, Psychology

Divorce was taboo in Japan in the 1970s, with divorced women thought of as inferior. In the United States divorce is more common than it is in many other countries. Have students research divorce rates worldwide, and create graphs and charts to display the countries' divorce rates.

97 Morressy, John, *The Juggler.*

Holt, 1996, 261pp. $16.95. ISBN: 0-80-504217-2. HarperTrophy, 1998, 261pp. $4.95. ISBN: 0-06-447174-8
Subjects: The Devil, Magic, Middle Ages, Relationships
Genres: Historical, Horror
List: Author's Choice
Levels: BL 7–10, SLJ 7–12

Annotation: During the Middle Ages an orphaned young man bargains with the devil and agrees to give up his soul to be the world's best juggler. The juggler falls in love and no longer wants to keep his part of the bargain when the devil arrives to collect.

Booktalk: The juggler had entered the Count's lands without permission, but was not punished for his unauthorized entry because he pleased the Count with his juggling. However, when the juggler leaves the Count's lands without permission, he is brought back to be punished. The Count asks the juggler which of his hands he would prefer cut off. The juggler calmly says it does not matter to him. The Count chooses the right hand. The juggler is led away and the next day his right hand is chopped off, with the court physician in attendance. At no point during the punishment does the juggler struggle or complain. How puzzling. Why would the world's best juggler sit back and let one of his hands be severed at the wrist? Perhaps it has something to do with how he became the world's best juggler and his desire to no longer hold that title.

Curriculum Connection: English

Reviews of *The Juggler* refer to this novel as a Faustian tale. Have students research who Faust was and why this story of a young man bargaining his soul with the Devil is referred to as Faustian.

Myers, Walter Dean, *Fallen Angels*.

98

Scholastic, 1988, 320pp. $14.95. ISBN: 0-590-40942-5. Scholastic, 1988, 309pp. $4.99. ISBN: 0-590-40943-3
Subjects: African Americans, Brothers, Death, Friendship, Race Relations, Vietnam War, Violence, War
Genres: Historical, Multicultural
Lists: 2000 B of BBYA, 1998 PP
Award: Coretta Scott King
Level: SLJ 10 & Up

Annotation: Seventeen-year-old Richie Perry, an African American from Harlem, enlists in the army and survives a 1967 tour of duty in Vietnam, describing the terror of war and seeing his friends being killed on the battlefield.

Booktalk: Richie wanted out of Harlem, so he enlisted in the Army, but where he finds himself is a lot more dangerous than the streets of Harlem. After seeing what the Viet Cong did to a village and the people in it, Richie questions whether he should tell his little brother about what was really happening over there. One of his buddies tells him that he needs to tell his little brother it is like what he sees in the movies, because if Richie doesn't, no one will come and fight the next war. Is that what Richie should do, or should he tell his little brother the truth about the atrocities of war, about tiny babies being blown up and men being tortured? This war doesn't look like any movie he watched back home in Harlem.

Curriculum Connection: History
   The Vietnam War came into American homes every night via the evening news on television. Have students research and discuss the effect this immediacy of war had on American support of U.S. involvement in Vietnam.

Myers, Walter Dean, *Monster*.

99

HarperCollins, 1999, 281pp. $15.89. ISBN: 0-06-028078-6. HarperCollins, 2001, 288pp. $5.95. ISBN: 0-06-440731-4
Subjects: African Americans, Authorship, Fathers and Sons, Journal Writing, Murder
Genres: Multicultural, Realistic
Lists: 2000 BBYA, 2000 QP
Awards: Coretta Scott King, Michael L. Printz
Levels: BL 9–12, SLJ 7–12

Annotation: Sixteen-year-old Steve is in jail, on trial as an accomplice to a murder. To deal with his incarceration, Steve writes in his journal as well as creates a screenplay of his time behind bars and in the courtroom.

Booktalk: Is there ever a right time to not tell the truth? Steve is in jail, on trial as an accomplice to a murder, when he overhears another inmate saying that the prosecuting attorney said he was lying. The inmate wanted to know what did that prosecutor expect him to do—tell the truth? If he did that, he was sure to get 10 years in prison. He said that the truth didn't mean anything when you were facing time behind bars. Steve listened to what the guy was saying. Then he began to tell him that truth is truth and you should do what you know is right. But the other guy cut him off, telling him that truth was given up in the streets; in prison the only thing that mattered was survival. The question is: What will Steve do to survive?

Curriculum Connections: English, Psychology

Myers interviewed hundreds of incarcerated young men, and most of them blamed someone else, or life's circumstances, for why they were in prison. Have students discuss whether they think this is what Steve is doing in this book, blaming someone else and not taking responsibility for his part in the death of the shopkeeper.

100 Myers, Walter Dean, *Slam!*

Scholastic, 1996, 266pp. $15.95. ISBN: 0-590-48667-5. Scholastic, 1996, 266pp. $4.99. ISBN: 0-590-48668-3
Subjects: African Americans, Basketball, High Schools
Genres: Multicultural, Realistic, Sports
Lists: 2000 B of BBYA, 1999 PP, 1998 YAC, 1997 BBYA, 1997 QP
Award: Coretta Scott King Honor
Levels: BL 8–12, SLJ 8–12, VOYA 7–12

Annotation: Seventeen-year-old Slam's grades are sinking in his classes at Latimer Arts Magnet School in the Bronx, his grandmother is dying, his best friend is dealing cocaine, and his coach doesn't like his attitude on the court. Slam hopes his basketball talents will get him out of the inner city.

Booktalk: Slam got his name because that is exactly what he does with a basketball—he slam-dunks it. On the court, Slam has complete control of the ball and of the game—he has all the confidence in the world. Matter of fact, he is downright cocky. But take Slam off of the court and everything changes. He has no control of the game of life on the streets or in the classroom. Slam has to play one-on-one with life off the court—and he isn't so sure he is going to win.

Curriculum Connections: English, Psychology

Like Slam, we all have areas of our lives where we are in the most control. Have students write about their definition of "being in control" and the area of their life in which they feel most in control.

Namioka, Lensey, *Ties That Bind, Ties That Break.*

Delacorte, 1999, 154pp. $15.95. ISBN: 0-385-32666-1. Bantam Doubleday Dell, 2000, 160pp. $4.99. ISBN: 0-440-41599-3

Subjects: Chinese, Family Problems, Fathers and Daughters, Self-esteem
Genres: Historical, Multicultural
List: 2000 BBYA
Levels: BL 7–10, SLJ 7–10

Annotation: Nineteen-year-old Ailin, now the wife of a restaurant owner in San Francisco's Chinatown, recalls the effects on her life by her refusal to have her feet bound as a young child born of a wealthy family in Nanjing during the period of Revolution and change in China.

Booktalk: Ailin stopped to catch her breath when she saw his familiar face across the restaurant, the man with whom her family had arranged her marriage so many years ago when she was a young child in Nanjing, China. The painful memories of the way she was treated as a female with unbound feet came back—the broken marriage arrangement, the scorn of other well-bred men and women, and the ostracism by her own family. Then one memory rose above the others—the memory of the rotting smell when the maid began to unwrap her 16-year-old sister's bound feet and the sight of those tiny little stumps with the big toes sticking straight out, but the other toes deformed and folded under. It was clear, even to Ailin as a small child, that the only way for her sister's toes to be in that position was for them to be broken and forced under and held by the long strips of cloth that had been wrapped around her feet. Ailin shook away the memories and walked over, on her beautiful, big, unbound feet, to speak to the man she was glad she had not married.

Curriculum Connections: History, Sociology

For many generations the feet of Chinese women were bound. Even though the tiny lotus-shaped feet were considered a sign of beauty, by binding their feet the women became totally dependent upon their men. Have students research Chinese history in relation to the role of women in this culture.

102 Napoli, Donna Jo, *Beast.*

Atheneum, 2000, 260pp. $17. ISBN: 0-689-83589-2
Subjects: Fairies, Fathers and Daughters, Magic
Genres: Fantasy, Multicultural
List: Author's Choice
Levels: BL 7–10, VOYA 7–12

Annotation: In this Persian version of "Beauty and the Beast," a prince is changed into a lion by a fairy. The lion/prince journeys to France and finds a deserted castle, where he lives until a merchant picks roses from his garden. The merchant sends his daughter, Belle, to the castle, and she falls in love with the beast and breaks the spell.

Booktalk: The prince wakes up, hoping the curse was only a dream. He has to get to his bedroom and lock the door so his father won't kill him. Orasmyn tries to rise to his feet but can't. He looks down and is terrified to see a lion's body laid out in front of him. He knows his father is going to shoot the lion, it will jump out of the way, and the arrow will enter his heart. He tries to jump to his feet, and then he sees the lion's back and tail behind him. His heart is racing, but his terror has only begun. What Orasmyn will soon realize is that the pari (fairy) has turned him into a lion on the very day his father is to lead the royal lion hunt.

Curriculum Connection: English
Many retellings of well-known fairy tales have been published. Have students choose three versions of the same fairy tale, one of them a picture book version. Students then create a comparison chart of elements of the story that vary from one version to another, such as setting, sex of main character, and so on.

103 Nix, Garth, *Sabriel.*

HarperCollins, 1996, 292pp. $16.95. ISBN: 0-06-027322-4. HarperTrophy, 1997. $5.95. ISBN: 0-06-447183-7
Subjects: Death, Fathers and Daughters, Magic, Self-esteem
Genre: Fantasy
Lists: 1997 BBYA, 2000 B of BBYA
Levels: BL 7–12, SLJ 6 & Up

Annotation: Seventeen-year-old Sabriel returns to the Old Kingdom to find her father's body and to bring him back from The Land of the Dead so he can help her destroy the evil being that is destroying the kingdom.

Booktalk: Sabriel wore the garb of the Abhorsen and carried the bells that rang the dead back to sleep next to the sword swirling with charter marks. But she still felt like she was merely the daughter of the real Abhorsen, not his replacement. Her father had been lured into the Land of the Dead by the evil being that had once been a prince of the Old Kingdom. Even though Sabriel was unsure of herself as the Abhorsen, she was sure it was time to return to the Old Kingdom, walk into the Land of the Dead, find her father, and bring him back long enough to help her defeat the evil prince.

Nix, Garth, *Shade's Children.* | 104

HarperCollins, 1997, 288pp. $15.89. HarperTrophy, 1998, 345pp. $5.95. ISBN: 0-06-447196-9
Subjects: Extraterrestrial Beings, Friendship, Medical Experimentation, War
Genre: Science Fiction
List: 1998 BBYA
Levels: BL 7–12, SLJ 9 & Up

Annotation: Ella, Drum, Ninde, and Gold-Eye are part of Shade's young army who are battling the Overlords, aliens who kill human children when they turn 14, and harvest their brains and muscles to construct creatures whose sole purpose is to kill.

Booktalk: Gold-Eye has escaped from the meat factory, but he is running out of time and the energy to avoid capture by the Wingers, Trackers, Myrmidons, and Ferrets sent out by the Overlords. Just when he is sure he has run out of time and luck, a rope drops down from the top of a wall and he is pulled to safety, only to come face to face with two females and a male dressed for battle. But there is no time for small talk. The Trackers are hot on their trail. Gold-Eye doesn't know it yet, but he has just become one of Shade's Children.

Nixon, Joan Lowery, *The Haunting.* | 105

Delacorte, 1998, 184pp. $15.95. ISBN: 0-385-32247-X. Bantam Doubleday Dell, 2000, 192pp. $4.99. ISBN: 0-440-22008-4
Subjects: Ghosts, Murder, Parent and Child
Genres: Mystery, Supernatural
Lists: 2000 YAC, 1999 QP
Levels: BL 6–10, SLJ 7–10

Annotation: The mother of 15-year-old Lia inherits a haunted Louisiana mansion. Lia uses the clues in Poe's short stories to figure out that the Civil War-era owner had killed the unscrupulous overseer and hidden his body in a bricked-over area of the basement. Lia finds the overseer's skeleton and releases both ghosts.

Booktalk: Lia's relatives have been paying for the upkeep of Graymoss for generations, but no one will live in it. The whole town knows the mansion is haunted by evil spirits. When Lia's mother inherits it and wants to live in the house, everyone thinks she is crazy. Lia's mother thinks the ghost story is hysteria based on a Civil War-era diary found in the house, but Lia knows that the ghosts are real. Why else would a copy of *Favorite Tales of Edgar Allan Poe* fly out of the bookcase and hit her in the shoulder? Her ancestors hadn't figured out the connection to Poe, but Lia is intent on finding out why a vengeful ghost is haunting Graymoss and what it has to do with Edgar Allan Poe.

Curriculum Connection: English

The answer to the mystery of who is haunting Graymoss is found in Poe's short story "The Cask of Amontillado." Have the students read the short story before they read *The Haunting* and discuss their theories of how this short story will relate to the book. Can they solve the mystery before Lia does?

106 Nolan, Han, *Dancing on the Edge.*

Harcourt Brace, 1997, $16. ISBN: 0-15-201648-1. Penguin Putnam, 1999, 256pp. $5.99. ISBN: 0-14-130203-8
Subjects: Fathers and Daughters, Grandparents, Mental Illness
Genre: Realistic
List: 1998 BBYA
Levels: BL 7–10, SLJ 6 & Up

Annotation: Miracle McCloy, named Miracle because she was delivered after her mother died, is trying to psychically contact her father. Grandmother Gigi claims he "melted" and can't be found, but Miracle keeps trying until she sets herself on fire with candles, thus getting the psychiatric help she needs. 1997 National Book Award Winner.

Booktalk: Miracle received her name because she was delivered after her mother was dead, having been hit by a bus. Her reclusive father and eccentric grandmother have raised her since her miraculous birth. But now Miracle's father has disappeared, and her grandmother Gigi is not helping Miracle understand what has happened to him. She tells her that he just melted. Miracle wants to know how that is possible. Gigi is so deep into her mystical lifestyle that she doesn't notice that her granddaughter is dancing on the edge of sanity—that is, until Miracle dons her father's bathrobe and steps into a ring of lit candles trying to "melt" like her father did. The bathrobe catches fire from the candles and Miracle begins to "melt." But this melting is not miraculous. It is painful, both physically and emotionally.

Curriculum Connections: Health, Psychology

The terminology surrounding death can be quite confusing for young people. They may be asked, "When did you lose your father?" Have students brainstorm the terms we use rather than "dead" or "died." Have them discuss whether they think using these terms helps young people understand that when someone dies they do not come back.

Orr, Wendy, *Peeling the Onion.* | 107

Holiday House, 1997, 166pp. $16.95. ISBN: 0-8234-1289-X. Bantam Doubleday Dell, 1999, 166pp. $4.99. ISBN: 0-4402-2773-9

Subjects: Accidents, Emotional Problems, Physically Handicapped
Genre: Realistic
Lists: 2000 B of BBYA, 1998 BBYA
Levels: BL 8–12, SLJ 6 & Up

Annotation: The life of 17-year-old Anna revolved around karate until an automobile accident ended that part of her life. She spends the next year in great pain because a rural Australian doctor incorrectly diagnosed her neck injury. The pain is not all physical; Anna has to redefine her future based on the irreversible physical handicaps resulting from a broken neck.

Booktalk: One second Anna is on cloud nine coming home from a karate competition; the next second she wakes up in an ambulance remembering screeching tires and flying glass. Her broken thumb is throbbing, but what she is feeling in her neck is beyond pain. She feels like her neck has been shredded, that she is being strangled, and the spasms of pain shooting through the torn tissue is beyond excruciating. It is a level of pain she has never felt. Anna is not sure she can bear this pain any further. What she doesn't know is that this is only the beginning of the pain, both physical and emotional.

Curriculum Connection: Physical Education

Athletes often get injured on or off the court or field to the degree that they cannot play their sport of choice ever again. Have students discuss alternatives to playing the sport to keep actively involved.

108 Paulsen, Gary, *Sarny: A Life Remembered.*

Delacorte, 1997, 180pp. $15.95. ISBN: 0-385-32195-3. Bantam Doubleday Dell, 1999, 192pp. $4.99. ISBN: 0-440-219373-6

Subjects: African Americans, Civil War, Parent and Child, Slavery, Teachers, War
Genres: Historical, Multicultural
Lists: 1999 YAC, 1998 QP
Levels: BL 6–12, SLJ 6–10

Annotation: Sarny searches for her children, who had been sold just before the Civil War ended. She eventually finds them in New Orleans, where she begins her new life working for Ms. Laura, a woman who entertains wealthy men. Sarny learns to read, and later opens schools to teach other African Americans to read. Companion novel to *Nightjohn* (Delacorte, 1993).

Booktalk: Sarny had finally gotten to the deserted slave yard where she hoped she would find her children, but all she found was the wagon and chains in which they had been taken away. Then she heard a sound like a hammer hitting meat to soften it, and she ran into the main yard to see what it was. She saw Greerson, the slave trader, who had taken her children, but it was too late for him to tell her where her children were. Greerson's eyes were rolled back in his head, but the black man just kept beating him, saying he was giving Greerson back what he had given him when he'd been whipped. Sarny turned away from the gruesome scene with tears in her eyes, not for Greerson, but for her children. How was she going to find them now?

Curriculum Connection: History

Sarny does find her children and eventually becomes a teacher, opening many schools for blacks. However, not all of the blacks in the South were so fortunate. After the Civil War, many of the freed blacks had no skills other than fieldwork. Have students research the Reconstruction Period after the Civil War in relation to working conditions for blacks in the South.

Paulsen, Gary, *Soldier's Heart.* — 109

Delacorte, 1998, 106pp. $15.95. ISBN: 0-385-32498-7. Bantam Doubleday Dell, 2000, 128pp. $5.50. ISBN: 0-440-22838-7

Subjects: Civil War, Mental Illness, War
Genre: Historical
Lists: 2002 PP, 2000 B of BBYA, 1999 BBYA, 1999 QP
Levels: BL 5–8, SLJ 7 & Up

Annotation: Fifteen-year-old Charley enlists in the First Minnesota Volunteers during the Civil War, experiences the fear and excitement of battle, and returns home with Soldier's Heart, now known as post-traumatic stress syndrome.

Booktalk: Charley listened to the men talking about signing up for the First Minnesota Volunteers. He wanted to go to war as a man and send home the $11 a month to his mother. He knew they would never take him if they knew he was 15, so he changed his birth certificate to make himself 18 and signed up anyway. Charley soon learned, along with the boredom of waiting, the abject terror of battle. Marching across a meadow toward the Rebels, knowing a bullet could hit him at any moment, was almost more than Charley could bear. He looked down and realized he had wet his pants. Looking around, he realized so had many of the other soldiers. Charley thought he was going to die any moment, but dying would have been easier than what Charley was in for.

Curriculum Connection: History

After each war in which Americans have fought, soldiers have experienced post-traumatic stress syndrome. It was called Soldier's Heart after the Civil War. Have students research what this syndrome was called after World War I, World War II, the Korean War, and the Vietnam War.

Peck, Richard, *The Last Safe Place on Earth.* — 110

Bantam Doubleday Dell, 1996, 161pp. $3.99. ISBN: 0-440-22007-6

Subjects: Censorship, High Schools, Relationships, Religion
Genre: Realistic
Lists: 1997 PP, 1996 BBYA, 1996 QP
Levels: BL 7–10, SLJ 6–10

Annotation: Fifteen-year-old Todd thinks he has found the girl of his dreams until he discovers that Laurel belongs to a religious group that is trying to censor books from the high school library and that she believes Halloween is evil, scaring his little sister with her religious zealousness.

Booktalk: Todd didn't want to believe Laurel had anything to do with Marnie's behavior. Halloween was a big holiday for their family, with Marnie joyously wearing her witch costume. But instead of celebrating, little Marnie cut up her costume and tried to flush it down the toilet. When Todd asked his little sister why she had cut up her costume, Marnie told him it was evil. Later, Todd stood in stunned silence when Laurel proudly announced that she had told Marnie that witches were real and that they worshipped the devil. She insisted she was only trying to save Marnie because clearly Marnie's family couldn't. Todd was still at a loss for words when his mother escorted Marnie's babysitter through their front door, asking her to never return. How could he have been so wrong about Laurel? He had even thought she was going to be his girlfriend.

Curriculum Connections: English, History

Censorship has been present as long as the printed word. Have students research the history of censorship, as well as current censorship issues. They should choose and read a past or recently censored book and discuss why this particular book had been censored.

111 Powell, Randy, *Dean Duffy.*

Farrar, Straus & Giroux, 1995, 170pp. $15. ISBN: 0-374-31754-2. Farrar, Straus & Giroux, 1998, 176pp. $4.95. ISBN: 0-374-41699-0

Subjects: Baseball, Self-esteem
Genres: Realistic, Sports
Lists: 1996 BBYA, 1996 QP
Levels: BL 8–12, SLJ 7 & Up

Annotation: Graduated from high school and thinking he had ruined any chances of a career in baseball, the once star pitcher and batter Dean Duffy is searching for answers in his life. He has to decide whether he is going to lower his initial expectations and accept a trial baseball scholarship at a small private college.

Booktalk: By ninth grade Dean was six foot three. By tenth he was six foot four—tall enough to make college scouts and even pro scouts take him seriously. Even though he was still in junior high, he was brought up to the high school varsity team. He mowed them down with fastballs, forkballs, and wicked curves. When it was his turn at bat, he slugged the ball out of there. In his sophomore year he got a card from the University of Washington with a gold R on a purple background to stand for Recruit. That same year the major league scouts came to watch Dean strike out 10 batters per game, hit .587, and be the only sophomore chosen for the Seattle Times High School All-State Team. But then the dream died and now, at age 18 and no longer in high school, Dean is trying to figure out what happened to his winning streak and what he will do with his life.

Curriculum Connection: Physical Education

Many high school athletes are sure that they will be offered a sports scholarship to a particular college, just as Dean Duffy was until his winning streak stopped. Have students discuss the actual potential of college or professional offers for most high school sports stars.

112 Preston, Douglas, and Lincoln Child, *The Relic.*

Tor, 1996, 474pp. $6.99. ISBN: 0-8125-4326-2
Subject: Murder
Genres: Horror, Mystery
Lists: 2000 PP, 1996 BBYA
Level: Adult

Annotation: Visitors and employees of the New York City Museum of Natural History are being savagely murdered in the hallways and secret rooms of the museum by a beast created in the Amazon jungle. Doctoral student Margo Green tracks down the beast. Companion novel to *Reliquary* (Tor, 1998).

Booktalk: Even though he knows a creature is savagely murdering people in the New York Museum of Natural History, the director ignores the warnings and proceeds with the gala for the new exhibition area. He gets more excitement than he bargains for as the creature takes life after life. The creature is so cunning it even takes out the FBI's SWAT team. The beast appears to have humanlike thought processes. It knows exactly what it is doing. The museum scientists seem to think that it cannot be stopped. But there is one person who just might have the answer to how to kill it—she just doesn't know it yet.

113 Qualey, Marsha, *Come in from the Cold.*

Houghton Mifflin, 1994, 219pp. $15.95. ISBN: 0-395-68986-4
Subjects: Brothers and Sisters, Relationships, Vietnam War, Vietnam War Protests
Genre: Historical, Romance
List: 1996 YAC
Levels: BL 9–12, SLJ 8–12

Annotation: In 1969, the Vietnam War is raging when 17-year-old Maud, sister of a radical protester who died in a bombing, and Jeff, brother of a Marine who died in combat, meet, fall in love, and join a commune.

Booktalk: Maud was picking up beer cans and cigarette butts at the beach party when she straightened up and was face to face with a girl. Maud smiled and said, "Hello." The girl totally took her by surprise when she shook up a can of beer and popped it open right into her face. Beer ran off the tip of Maud's nose. The girl told her that her brother was killed in Vietnam last March. Maud said she was sorry. But she knew what was coming next. The girl wanted to know if the woman the FBI wanted, the one who poured paint on the President's car and shot two police officers in Chicago, was her sister. Maud said her sister didn't shoot anyone, she had only bought the guns. The girl slapped her across the face and shouted that Maud's sister should be dead, not her brother. But Maud didn't want Lucy dead, she just wanted to know if she was dead or alive.

Curriculum Connection: History

As far back as the Revolutionary War, Americans have had differing views on U.S. involvement in a war. Compare the viewpoints of the war oppositionists from the Revolutionary War and the Civil War with those of the Vietnam War protesters. Did they have any viewpoints in common?

114 Randle, Kristen D., *The Only Alien on the Planet.*

Scholastic, 1995. $4.99. ISBN: 0-590-46310-1
Subjects: Brothers, Child Abuse, Friendship, Mental Illness
Genre: Realistic
Lists: 1999 PP, 1996 BBYA, 1996 QP
Levels: BL 8–12, SLJ 8 & Up

Annotation: Ginny, the new girl in town, reaches out in friendship to Smitty, the boy they call "The Alien" because he never speaks. Smitty's older brother had abused him, almost killing Smitty when he was two, and told him he would die if he ever spoke of it. The young boy quit speaking altogether, until Ginny brings him out of his self-imposed silence.

Booktalk: Ginny saw him in the back of the classroom—the most beautiful guy she had ever seen. They said Smitty was autistic, or something, and everyone called him "The Alien." But when she asked Caulder about Smitty, he said he knew he was in there somewhere, even though he had never heard Smitty speak. His comment made Ginny think about her grandmother when she was in the nursing home before she died. Everyone thought that because her body was out of control, her mind was gone too. Ginny now wondered if her grandmother had been trapped in there somewhere, thinking her own thoughts. And Ginny kept thinking about how that might be the case with Smitty. He might be trapped behind that angelic face, somewhere. Maybe she could help him open the trap door. But Ginny had no idea what demons were behind that tightly closed door. Only silent Smitty—and his older brother—knew.

Reuter, Bjarne, *The Boys from St. Petri.*

Dutton, 1994, 215pp. $14.99. ISBN: 0-525-45121-8. Penguin Putnam, 1996, 192pp. $5.99. ISBN: 0-140-37994-0

Subjects: Brothers, Gangs, War, World War II
Genre: Historical
List: 2002 PP
Level: BL 7–10

Annotation: In 1942, two teenage Danish brothers and their friends start out playing pranks on the Nazis occupying their small town. But the pranks turn into more serious resistance.

Booktalk: Fraternities have initiations. Gangs have initiations. But did you ever think of an initiation taking place as far back as 1942, and in a church at that? That's exactly what happened to Lars. He wanted to join the Boys of St. Petri—the "gang" that stole Nazi hats from cafes and license plates from their cars, and harassed them in any way they could. Gunnar, Lars' brother, led the group and warned him that the initiation was not going to be easy. They would tie a rope around him and then they would pull the peg out. Lars had no idea how excruciating the pain was going to be when they pulled the peg out. He could taste the blood in his mouth and the rope was burning the palms of his hands. He could only nod when he was asked if he swore that he would never accept Nazi Germany's invasion of Denmark. He would have sworn anything to get them to put that peg back in.

Curriculum Connection: History

When we think of World War II, we typically think of the German occupation of Poland and France, and of the Germans' relentless bombing of England. Have students do research on the lesser-known countries that the Nazis occupied and the role of the resistance fighters in these smaller countries, such as Denmark and Norway.

116 Rosenberg, Joel, *Not Exactly the Three Musketeers.*

(The Guardians of the Flame series, #8) Tor, 1999, 316pp. $23.95. ISBN: 0-312-85782-9. Tor, 2000, 325pp. $6.99. ISBN: 0-812-55046-3

Subjects: Dragons, Friendship, Magic
Genre: Fantasy
List: Author's Choice
Level: Adult

Annotation: The three heroes of the Castle Cullinane set out to rescue a noble woman who they think is being forced into marriage, and end up rescuing the royal dragon with the help of a wizard.

Booktalk: Have you ever gotten involved in a role-playing game, such as Dungeons and Dragons? Well, many of the readers of Rosenberg's *Guardians of the Flame* series have. They like Rosenberg's books because he writes so descriptively you feel like you are in the book. You may be surprised to look down and realize you don't have a sword in your hand, like Kethol, or an ax, like Durine. You go right into battle with them as they rescue damsels in distress and assist a wizard as he becomes a decoy for a marauding dragon. Not only do these heroes carry deadly weapons, which they use with regularity, they are created by an author with a wickedly sharp sense of humor. Who else but Rosenberg would talk about how difficult it is to keep sphincter control at the sight of a dragon with teeth like jagged yellow swords and breath that reeks of sulfur?

Curriculum Connection: English

Many of the fantasy novels that high school students read are marketed for adult readers. Many of these novels are part of a series, as *Not Exactly the Three Musketeers* is the eighth novel in the *Guardians of the Flame* series. Divide students into groups of four or five and have them pick an adult fantasy series to read and discuss. Each member of the group randomly chooses a different book without knowing which number in the series it is. After the members read their books, they discuss whether they felt they were missing out on the whole story because they hadn't read the entire series. Have the students share their impressions of the series through a booktalk or a general discussion with the rest of the class. After each group has discussed their series, have them compile a list of similar elements among the various series.

Seymour, Tres, *The Revelation of Saint Bruce.*

117

Orchard, 1998, 120pp. $16.95. ISBN: 0-531-33109-1
Subjects: Friendship, High Schools, Religion
Genre: Realistic
List: Author's Choice
Levels: BL 7–12, SLJ 7 & Up

Annotation: Seventeen-year-old Bruce is an honest, religious, and often quite righteous individual who chooses to tell the truth when asked about his friends drinking in school, and suffers the consequences of betraying their trust.

Booktalk: Bruce was out of school for a week with the flu. It was during his absence that his friends had decided to share a bottle of Jack Daniels, at the expense of the naïve substitute teacher who left them in the classroom alone. On Bruce's first day back, they piled into his car and headed out of the senior lot. They were trying to get him to burn rubber, which they knew was about as likely as "Saint Bruce" running naked through the cafeteria during lunch period. Then Ellis tapped him on the shoulder and told Bruce he should have been with them Friday afternoon. Bruce knew from his friend's tone of voice that he didn't want to hear this. As soon as he heard the word "party," he knew he really didn't want to hear anymore, but they kept talking. Bruce couldn't very well put his hands over his ears; he was driving down the middle of the road. But now he knew. It was their own fault for telling him. They were about to find out what a big mistake it was to tell him what they had done.

Curriculum Connections: English, Government
   Each of the chapters of this novel is prefaced by passages from the Bible. Have students discuss the concept of separation of church and state as well as the Supreme Court ruling that the Bible can be used in schools as literature.

Shoup, Barbara, *Stranded in Harmony.*

118

Hyperion, 1997, 188pp. $17.95. ISBN: 0-7868-0287-1. Disney Press, 2001, 224pp. $5.99. ISBN: 0-7868-1501-9
Subjects: The Elderly, Football, Friendship, Sexual Relationships, Vietnam War Protests
Genre: Realistic
Lists: 1999 YAC, 1998 BBYA
Levels: BL 7–10, SLJ 6 & Up

Annotation: During his senior year of high school, Lucas meets and becomes friends with a Vietnam War protester who spent time in prison for murder after a bombing. Lucas discovers that there is more to life than football and dating a cheerleader.

Booktalk: Did you have a favorite book when you were a little kid? Lucas' favorite book was *Where the Wild Things Are* (HarperCollins, 1988), and he remembered the day his mother came in and found him jumping up and down on the book, open to the center page. She reprimanded him for mistreating his book, but what he was trying to do was to get inside the story. It was happening to Lucas again, getting into the story—but this time it was real. He was sitting in the library with bits and pieces of Allie's life all around him in books. There were pictures of a young Allie and the man she was with when they set off the bomb. There was a picture of his body lying in a pool of blood and another of Allie being led away in hand cuffs. Seeing Allie with her hands hiding her face as she was being taken to jail made his research on the Vietnam War protests all too real.

Curriculum Connection: History

Although *Stranded in Harmony* is set in the contemporary Midwest, the main character is doing research on the Vietnam War era. He becomes wrapped up in the time period because he's doing his research through more than books. Have students choose an incident in recent history that they can interview someone about, as well as do print and electronic research.

119 Shusterman, Neal, *Downsiders*.

Simon & Schuster, 1999, 246pp. $16.95. ISBN: 0-689-80375-3. Aladdin, 2001, 244pp. $4.99. ISBN: 0-689-83969-3
Subjects: Friendship, Survival
Genre: Science Fiction
Lists: 2002 PP, 2000 BBYA, 2000 QP
Level: SLJ 8 & Up

Annotation: Beneath New York City lies a secret world called the Downside, which had been created by an architect many years before. Fourteen-year-old Talon and the rest of the Downsiders do not know this. They think their civilization has always been there. The two worlds collide when Talon does the forbidden and takes a Topsider into their world.

Booktalk: Talon knew Downsiders could go to the Topside only at night, and then only into the subways to catch fallers. Fallers had to shed all their clothing and any other belongings to enter the Downside. They had to swear never again to return to the light. But the girl Talon took into the tunnels beneath Manhattan was no faller. She wasn't trying to end her life, but she was very anxious to enter the Downside. Talon's stories of the Downside fascinated her, so Talon could not resist showing her his world. This transgression on Talon's part, if he got caught with her in the Downside, would result in his death sentence. Was Talon willing to take the risk?

Curriculum Connections: History, Sociology

There is some historical evidence of the existence of underground structures in the city of New York. Have students discuss the possibility of people like the Downsiders. Could they really exist in the subways of New York City and other large cities in the United States? Or is this science fiction, only possible in the future?

Sleator, William, *House of Stairs*.

Puffin, 1991, 166pp. $5.99. ISBN: 0-14-034580-9
Subjects: Friendship, Medical Experimentation, Self-esteem
Genre: Science Fiction
List: Author's Choice
Levels: No current interest levels available

Annotation: Five 16-year-old orphans are blindfolded and taken to a place that is built of nothing but stairs and small landings. They are unwilling participants in psychological experimentation on behavior modification.

Booktalk: Imagine finding yourself in a place with four other people your age that you don't know, stranded on an interconnecting maze of stairs with only small platforms between them. On one of the landings is a machine that dispenses brown pellets of food. On a narrow platform is a bowl of swirling water that you have to use as a toilet and for drinking water. Would you become friends with the others? Or would being confined to the stairs with little food and no privacy result in a battle of wits and strength? Would you go insane? Could you survive? And if you did, what would your mental state be like if they ever let you out?

Curriculum Connection: Psychology

What occurs to the five teenagers in this book is called behavior modification. Have students research the theory behind behavior modification and take a stand on whether they think it is ethical to modify people's behavior through punishment or rewards.

121 Soto, Gary, **Buried Onions.**

Harcourt Brace, 1997, 149pp. $17. ISBN: 0-15-201333-4. HarperTrophy, 1999. 160pp. $11. ISBN: 0-06-440771-3
Subjects: Death, Family Problems, Gangs, Mexican Americans, Violence
Genres: Multicultural, Realistic
Lists: 2002 PP, 1998 QP, 1998 BBYA
Levels: BL 8–12, SLJ 9 & Up

Annotation: After 19-year-old Eddie drops out of college, he finds life to be difficult in the violent Mexican-American Fresno barrio in which he lives. His aunt wants him to avenge his cousin's murder, his friend gets shot, and his employer's truck is stolen while Eddie has it.

Booktalk: Eddie can smell them—the buried onions of sadness and violence. They are beneath the black asphalt of his Mexican-American neighborhood in Fresno, California. You can see the burning vapors from those onions rising up from the asphalt. The smell makes babies scrunch up their little faces and cry as their mothers push them down the street in their strollers. It is why Eddie's neighbors have tears glistening on their eyelashes and staining their cheeks. It is why Eddie's family wants him to seek revenge for his cousin's death. But Eddie is tired of smelling the buried onions and is trying to find a way out of Fresno. He is willing to do just about anything to escape.

122 Stoehr, Shelly, **Tomorrow Wendy: A Love Story.**

Delacorte, 1998, 166pp. $15.95. ISBN: 0-385-32339-5
Subjects: Drug Abuse, Homosexuality, Mental Illness, Music, Sexual Relationships
Genre: Realistic
List: Author's Choice
Levels: K 9 & Up, SLJ 9 & Up

Annotation: This book is a candid view of the drug abuse and sexual activities of a teenage subculture, including 17-year-old Cary, her boyfriend, Danny, and his sister. Cary is questioning her sexuality because of her infatuation with Danny's sister.

Booktalk: Cary is so mixed up she doesn't know what to do. She goes home with Danny after school, even though she knows exactly what he wants. What she wants is for him to fall asleep so she can sneak into his sister's room to feel close to her. Cary is infatuated with Wendy, an infatuation so strong that she picks up one of Wendy's sweaters and buries her face in it to inhale her smell. Sound weird? Cary's life is even weirder than that. Her friend Rad shows up at the most stressful times of her life and gives her advice. She can even pick up the phone and dial a random number, and he will answer it. His advice is always in the form of lyrics that he sings to her. When Cary asks him to explain himself, he disappears or the phone goes dead. Can Cary survive if both Rad and Wendy disappear from her life?

Strasser, Todd, *Give a Boy a Gun.*

Simon & Schuster, 2000, 146pp. $16. ISBN: 0-689-81112-8

Subjects: High Schools, Self-esteem, Suicide, Violence
Genre: Realistic
List: Author's Choice
Levels: BL 6–12, SLJ 8 & Up

Annotation: Armed with stolen semi-automatic rifles, two high school sophomores terrorize a gymnasium full of students while seeking revenge against the football players and teachers who tormented them.

Booktalk: My name is Allison Findley. Even though I went out with Gary for almost two years, I wasn't the one closest to him. He had this thing going with Brendan, like their own online language, with conversations I wasn't allowed to be a part of, conversations about what they would do to the jocks and the teachers if they had a chance. One night when Gary wasn't around, I went drinking and cruising with Brendan. He wanted to drive the back roads. When I heard the first bang, I thought it was a tire, but then I saw the gun and smelled the burned gunpowder as he shot out all the lights at the railroad crossing and loaded a second clip. I never said a word. I didn't stop him. At the time I actually thought it was a little cool. I had no idea what he was practicing for.

Curriculum Connections: Psychology, Sociology

School violence became too real with the Columbine shooting. There have always been divided groups of teens in schools. Teens know what groups are present, but do they know which group they belong to and which ones they should stay away from? Have students choose one of the chapters in this book and relate their school experience to how the character is feeling.

Sweeney, Joyce, *Free Fall.*

Delacorte, 1996, 229pp. $15.95. ISBN: 0-385-32211-9. Bantam Doubleday Dell, 1997, 240pp. $4.50. ISBN: 0-440-21975-2

Subjects: Brothers, Death, Friendship, Survival
Genres: Adventure, Realistic
List: 1997 QP
Levels: BL 9–12, SLJ 7–10

Annotation: Two brothers and their best friends are trapped in a Florida cave for 24 hours and learn to work together to survive while they sort through conflicts from their past.

Booktalk: Neil was the older brother. He was supposed to be able to take care of things, but they were trapped in a cave and no one knew they were here. When he came around the corner and found the initials that he had carved into the wall what seemed like hours ago, he lost it. Anger and fear erupted inside of him like a blood storm. He threw himself against the wall and began to slam his hand against the rocks over and over. He drove his knee into the wall as if it were a door that was jammed. He heard a high-pitched screaming, a screaming that wouldn't stop. He then realized the screaming was coming from him and he couldn't stop it.

Curriculum Connections: English, Psychology

Neil suffers from claustrophobia while they are trapped in the cave. He cannot deal with being confined in small places. Have students choose a phobia to research, defining what the phobia means and discussing the way people with this phobia behave and appropriate ways to control it.

125 Sweeney, Joyce, *The Spirit Window.*

Bantam Doubleday Dell, 1999, 256pp. $4.50. ISBN: 0-440-22711-9
Subjects: Death, Ecology, Fathers and Daughters, Grandparents, Photography
Genres: Multicultural, Realistic, Supernatural
List: 1999 BBYA
Levels: BL 7–12, SLJ 6–10

Annotation: Fifteen-year-old photographer Miranda and her father and stepmother visit her grandmother in Florida, where the feud between her father and grandmother resumes because grandmother refuses to sell her property. When Miranda's grandmother dies, she leaves her property to the 18-year-old Native-American gardener, whom Miranda loves.

Booktalk: Miranda and Adam made their way through the swamp to a sacred place. Suddenly a window appeared in the blackness, and Miranda saw her grandmother Lila, who smiled and held out her hand to her. Before Miranda could react, the window disappeared and she found herself in her childhood playroom. There was her mother pouring jasmine tea for a little girl—herself. Miranda leaned forward to watch closely and saw the freckles on her mother's arms, the gypsy curls around her face, and her green eyes. Yes, she remembered now—her mother had green eyes. She had forgotten. Before she could reach out to her mother, she was back on the swamp mound with Adam. Miranda had had a vision through the spirit window, a vision that reinforced the strong connection she had with this place and her family. There was no way she was going to let her father sell the family home that had meant so much to her grandmother.

Curriculum Connection: Science

Developers want to buy the Florida Everglades property of Miranda's grandmother. Through the years many acres of these swamplands have been filled in for development. Have students research what has happened to the wildlife of Florida because of this development.

Sykes, Shelley, *For Mike.*

Delacorte, 1998, 197pp. $15.95. ISBN: 0-385-32337-9. Laureleaf, 2000, 208pp. $4.99. ISBN: 0-440-22693-7
Subjects: Death, Friendship, Ghosts, Religion
Genres: Mystery, Supernatural
List: Author's Choice
Level: BL 7–10

Annotation: After Mike disappears during their senior year in high school, Jeff keeps having dreams about Mike asking Jeff to find him. Jeff eventually solves the mystery of how Mike died—trying to stop a friend who was involved in dealing drugs.

Booktalk: Jeff knew it was a dream, but it was so real and in some ways welcome. He could hear his best friend, Mike, calling to him for help. He knew, if he kept going around the corners in his dream, that he would see Mike and he could ask him where he had been for the last three weeks. When Mike finally appeared in Jeff's dream, half of his face was in shadows, and his clothes were damp. Mike kept asking Jeff to come get him, but when Jeff asked him where he was, Mike answered by saying he was nowhere and that "it" was missing. When Jeff reached for his wrist, Mike backed away, out of his reach. In seconds Jeff was awake and sitting up in bed. For the last two nights, Jeff had had the same dream. He knew Mike needed help. Jeff was going to find his missing best friend one way or another.

Curriculum Connection: Psychology

Dreams are a way for people to deal with psychological issues in their lives. Psychologists use dream interpretation in therapy. Have students research dream interpretation and discuss whether they think this is an effective practice.

127 Taylor, Theodore, *The Bomb.*

Harcourt Brace, 1995, 197pp. $15. ISBN: 0-15-200867-5. Morrow/Avon, 1997, 176pp. $4.95. ISBN: 0-380-72723-4
Subjects: Death, Ecology, Friendship, Grandparents
Genres: Historical, Multicultural
Lists: 1997 YAC, 1996 BBYA
Levels: BL 7–10, SLJ 6–10

Annotation: In 1946, 14-year-old Sorry Rinamu tries to save his home, Bikini Atoll, from American atomic testing, but dies in his canoe when he sets sail into the cove as the bomb is being dropped.

Booktalk: Sorry had a bad feeling about the American's promises about the other island to which his people were being moved. The U.S. military said they would have to leave their island and move to Rongerik for two years. Sorry didn't like the idea of moving to an island with a lagoon half the size of Bikini's. But it wasn't just the move that was bothering him; it was what would happen to his home after they dropped the bomb. Somehow, he had to stop this experiment. He was sure he knew what would work. He was sure the Americans wouldn't kill innocent villagers. Sorry, his friend Tara, and Grandfather Jonjen would, for sure, stop them from dropping the bomb by paddling out into the lagoon. The Americans would, for sure, see the red sail on his outrigger, know there were people down there, and stop the atomic bombing. Surely they would, wouldn't they?

Curriculum Connection: History
Theodore Taylor was in the South Pacific when the atomic bomb was dropped on Bikini Atoll. He saw the resulting devastation, and it affected him so much that he wrote this book. Have students do research to find out if the Bikini Atoll villagers were ever able to return to their home.

128 Temple, Frances, *The Ramsay Scallop.*

Orchard, 1994, 310pp. $17.95. ISBN: 0-531-06836-6. HarperTrophy, 1995, 320pp. $4.95. ISBN: 0-06-440601-6
Subjects: Middle Ages, Relationships, Religion
Genre: Historical
List: 1997 PP
Levels: BL 7–10, SLJ 8 & Up

Annotation: In 1299, 14-year-old Elenor and her betrothed, Lord Thomas, have second thoughts about their marriage. So the village priest sends them on a pilgrimage to Spain, where they meet travelers along the way who share their stories and help Eleanor and Thomas develop a bond.

Booktalk: Father Gregory listened to Eleanor's confessions and knew she was afraid to marry Lord Thomas. The tiny 14-year-old was afraid she would die in childbirth just like her mother had. And when Thomas came back from the Crusades, he no more wanted to marry Eleanor than she did him. Thomas considered her a little brat of a child. On top of that, the village women were unhappy to see the men they had been married or betrothed to come back eight years later. Many had formed new relationships. Friar Paul was now calling the children of the new marriages children of sin, and the village was in an uproar. But Father Gregory had a plan to save them all: Eleanor and Thomas would go, as chaste companions, on a pilgrimage to the shrine of St. James in Spain to atone for the villagers' sins. Only after the pilgrimage could they consummate their marriage, thus giving Eleanor and Thomas time to get to know each other and the many pilgrims they would meet on the way, as well as time for Friar Paul and the village to settle down.

Curriculum Connection: History

Along with knights from many other nations, Sir Thomas joyously joined the Crusades, answering the call of the Pope. He returned an embittered soldier. Instead of becoming part of an organized effort, the soldiers had been drawn into political skirmishes, working as hired killers, while desperately trying to believe in the cause of whoever paid them. Have students research what the Crusades were initially supposed to be and what they ended up becoming.

Thesman, Jean, *The Moonstones.* 129

Penguin Putnam, 2000, 208pp. $5.99. ISBN: 0-14-130809-5
Subjects: Family Problems, Mothers and Daughters
Genre: Realistic
List: 2000 YAC
Level: SLJ 8–10

Annotation: Fifteen-year-old Jane loses her mother's trust when she accompanies her on a trip to clear out Grandmother's house on Puget Sound in Washington. When her selfish cousin, Ricki, arrives, Jane goes against her better judgment and sneaks out at night with Ricki to meet local boys at the rundown amusement park.

Booktalk: When Ricki and Aunt Norma arrived at Grandmother's house, Jane took a trip on the wild side. She had never snuck out of the house at night, but Ricki made that old, rundown amusement park sound so exciting. Before Ricki had arrived, Jane had looked at the park from the bedroom window. It did seem as if it were alive, pushing back the darkness of Puget Sound, a darkness as black as the edge of the universe. The lights were whirling around and around, and music was playing, and she did know the gray-eyed boy she met in town would be there. So she snuck down the stairs with Ricki after their mothers were asleep, feeling both frightened and excited.

Curriculum Connection: History

Jane and Ricki ride the Ferris wheel with the boys they meet at the amusement park. The Carousel, like the Ferris wheel, is an integral part of an amusement park. Have students research the history and development of amusement parks, and the rides in them. For example, who invented the Ferris wheel and the roller coaster?

130 Thomas, Rob, *Rats Saw God.*

Simon & Schuster, 1996, 219pp. $17. ISBN: 0-689-80207-2. Aladdin, 1996, 208pp. $4.50. ISBN: 0-689-80777-5
Subjects: Authorship, Drug Abuse, Fathers and Sons, High Schools
Genre: Realistic
Lists: 2002 PP, 1997 BBYA, 1997 QP
Levels: BL 8–11, SLJ 9 & Up

Annotation: Eighteen-year-old Steve takes on the assignment of writing 100 pages to make up for the English credit he lacks so he can graduate. In the process, he works through his turbulent relationships with his astronaut father and his old girlfriend.

Booktalk: Steve hadn't been called to the counselor's office because he was stoned, like he thought. Instead the counselor tossed an envelope from the National Test Service across his desk at Steve. Steve just had to look—it was a press release identifying him as a National Merit finalist. The counselor had looked at Steve's records, saw he was one English credit short of passing, and now was offering him a "deal." If Steve wanted to graduate, he had two choices: He could go to summer school, or he could turn in a 100-page paper on a topic he knew something about. That night Steve sat down and began to type: "Houston, Freshman Year."

131 Thompson, Julian F., *The Grounding of Group 6.*

Holt, 1997, 291pp. $15.95. ISBN: 0-8050-5085-X
Subjects: Camping, Friendship, Gambling, Parent and Child, Survival
Genres: Adventure, Horror
List: Author's Choice
Levels: No current interest levels available

Annotation: Five 16-year-olds are sent to a private school, where their parents have paid for them to be murdered while they are on a survival outing. The college-age hit man cannot kill them and becomes part of the group as they try to elude the school authorities.

Booktalk: All of the members of Group 6 at Coldbrook Country School have been sent there by their parents. Immediately upon arrival at the remotely located school, they are sent out on a survival expedition with a leader; a bonding experience before they actually start their classes is what the school authorities said. Their leader, Nat, is a college student recruited particularly for this group and is using his pay for the job to pay off a gambling debt. Nat thought he could follow through on what he is being paid to do, but the longer he spends with this group of misfits, the more he begins to like them. He doesn't think he is capable of making sure that the members of Group 6 never find their way back to Coldbrook Country School.

132

Van Dijk, Lutz, *Damned Strong Love: The True Story of Willi G. and Stephan K.*

Holt, 1995, 138pp. $15.95. ISBN: 0-8050-3770-5
Subjects: Homosexuality, Jews, War, World War II
Genre: Historical, Multicultural
List: 1996 BBYA
Levels: BL 8-12

Annotation: Sixteen-year-old Stephan falls in love with a young Nazi soldier, Willi, during the Nazi Occupation of Poland. The Gestapo discovers their relationship and Stephan is arrested, tortured, and put in a concentration camp. Based on a true story.

Booktalk: On his 16th birthday, Stephan's older brother Molokai, who is involved in the Polish Resistance, took him to one of their hiding places where they could secretly drink together to celebrate his birthday. Then Molokai began to talk about his daydreams about girls. As Stephan listened to him, he realized that all the thoughts that Molokai had about women, he had about men. It all started to make sense to him. With both fear and joy, he realized what was different about him. Stephan was ready to fall in love when he met Willi, but he was still too naïve to realize the consequences of the letter he wrote to his Nazi boyfriend.

Curriculum Connection: History

The Nazis were killing not only Jews during World War II. Have students do research in relation to the other groups the Nazis were trying to exterminate, including homosexuals and gypsies.

133 Vande Velde, Vivian, **Companions of the Night.**

Harcourt Brace, 1995, 224pp. $17. ISBN: 0-15-200221-9. Bantam Doubleday Dell, 1996, 212pp. $4.99. 0-440-91147-8
Subjects: Brothers and Sisters, Kidnapping, Vampires
Genre: Horror
Lists: 2000 PP, 1996 BBYA, 1996 QP
Levels: BL 7–10, SLJ 6–10

Annotation: Sixteen-year-old Kerry unknowingly comes to the rescue of a vampire while returning to the laundromat to retrieve her little brother's stuffed koala bear. She continues helping him because her father and brother are kidnapped in retaliation, with the kidnappers thinking she also is a vampire.

Booktalk: Kerry was not at all happy about having to return to the laundromat in the middle of the night to get her little brother's koala bear. She certainly had no idea when she agreed to the late night rescue that she would be saving the "life" of a vampire. How was she to know that the good-looking guy they dragged into the laundromat—bleeding, with his hands tied behind his back—was a vampire? He looked just like one of the students from the local college. Kerry was about to find out how wrong first impressions can be.

134 Vande Velde, Vivian, **Never Trust a Dead Man.**

Harcourt Brace, 1999, 194pp. $17. ISBN: 0-15-201899-9. Bantam Doubleday Dell, 2001, 194pp. $4.99. ISBN: 0-44-022828-X
Subjects: Murder, Witchcraft
Genres: Humor, Mystery, Supernatural
Lists: 2000 BBYA, 2000 QP
Levels: BL 7–12, SLJ 6–9

Annotation: Seventeen-year-old Selwyn, buried in a tomb with the body of Farold, the man whom he supposedly killed, enlists the help of a witch to resurrect Farold so he can help Selwyn clear his name. But Selwyn makes a mistake, and Farold's soul enters the body of a bat. Together they solve the mystery of who killed Farold.

Booktalk: It's not like Selwyn knew how a resurrection spell worked. He hadn't met a witch before, and he honestly didn't know how important it was that the human leg bone he held was touching the dead body and not be moved. Nor did he know that, just as the witch was telling the soul to enter the body, that the bats would decide to take off into the night, startling him so that the leg bone momentarily pointed up at the ceiling. Selwyn didn't realize what had gone wrong until he heard the dead man's voice screaming many octaves too high from the body of a little bat. Even though it was Selwyn's fault that Farold had been turned into a bat, he could have been more appreciative than that! Didn't Farold want revenge against whoever had killed him?

Voigt, Cynthia, **When She Hollers.** 135

Scholastic, 1994, 177pp. $13.95. ISBN: 0-590-46714-X
Subjects: Child Sexual Abuse, Self-esteem, Stepfamilies
Genre: Realistic
List: Author's Choice
Levels: BL 7–12, SLJ 7 & Up

Annotation: Seventeen-year-old Tish keeps a knife in her boot to protect herself from a sexually abusive stepfather, but eventually tells a friend's father, a lawyer, what has been happening to her.

Booktalk: Tish has difficulty breathing, she has difficulty concentrating, but what she has the most difficulty with is pretending—pretending that what has been happening to her is just a very bad nightmare. She tries pretending that she is safe, but pretending isn't going to keep her safe from his attacks. She keeps pretending that she will find someone who will believe her if she tells them what is happening to her. But Tish doesn't trust any adult enough to tell them about being attacked. So Tish gets a knife, one of those big survival knives, and she keeps it in her boot. If no one else can protect her, Tish will protect herself. Next time he comes in, the knife comes out.

Wallace, Rich, **Wrestling Sturbridge.** 136

Knopf, 1996, 133pp. $16. ISBN: 0-679-87803-3. Random House, 1997, 133pp. $4.99. ISBN: 0-679-855-2
Subjects: Friendship, Self-esteem, Wrestling
Genre: Sports
Lists: 1999 PP, 1997 BBYA, 1997 QP
Levels: BL 9–12, SLJ 8 & Up

Annotation: Ben decides that he can't spend his last year in high school as second best on the mat. He has to challenge his best friend to a match that will prove who is the best wrestler on the team. But even after defeat, Ben is still a winner, knowing he has a future away from this small Pennsylvania town.

Booktalk: Ben knew for a long time that the coach had decided that his best friend, Al, was going to be the wrestling star on their team, and he was supposed to accept his role as "the best workout partner." Well, he had had enough of being second best, never knowing for sure whether he could be the best. His father told him to be patient, but his friend Digit kept reminding him that if he wanted it bad enough he had to take it. So now here he was, trying to take it from Al, who was beyond mad that he would even attempt such a thing. It was the third period, and the moment had arrived. Who would win this match?

137   Weaver, Will, *Farm Team.*

HarperCollins, 1995, 288pp. $14.89. ISBN: 0-06-023589-6. HarperTrophy, 1999, 279 pp. $4.95. ISBN: 0-06-447118-7
Subjects: Baseball, Fathers and Sons, Friendship
Genre: Sports
List: 1996 BBYA
Level: BL 7–12

Annotation: In the 1970s, when the father of 14-year-old Billy Bagg is put in jail, Billy has to give up playing baseball to run the family's Minnesota dairy farm until, with the help of his mother, he forms a baseball team right on the farm. Companion novel to *Striking Out* (HarperCollins, 1993) and *Hard Ball* (HarperCollins, 1998).

Booktalk: Randy Meyers sold Billy's mom a lemon, and his dad, Abner, was none too happy about it. Abner had his own way of dealing with cheaters. Pulling a D-6 Caterpillar on a lowboy, he picked up Billy from school. They pulled up to Meyers' A-1 car lot, and Abner fired that Cat up and ploughed right through that car lot. The police showed up, but that didn't stop Abner; he just swung the Cat around and took down the office as well. After he ground it into kindling wood, he turned off the Cat. He was just sitting up there on it when the sheriff walked up. When the sheriff asked Abner if he was having trouble with the Cat, maybe the steering hydraulics broke or something, Abner wouldn't take the easy way out. He just said, "Nope." Then the sheriff suggested that he might have lost control of the Cat. Abner wouldn't agree to that either. Billy knew, when the sheriff said he was taking his bullheaded father downtown, that his chances of playing summer baseball in town had just gone from slim to none.

Curriculum Connection: Sociology

Two of the players on Billy's farm team are the sons of a migrant farm worker. This book is set in Minnesota, not in Texas or California, locations we usually think of in relation to migrant farm workers. Have students do research on migrant farm working families and the locations they travel to during the year. Where do these families fit into the economy?

Weaver, Will, *Hard Ball.* 138

HarperCollins, 1998, 240pp. $15.89. ISBN: 0-06-027122-1. HarperTrophy, 1999. $4.95. ISBN: 0-06-447208-6
Subjects: Baseball, Fathers and Sons, Friendship
Genre: Sports
List: 1999 BBYA
Levels: BL 7–12, SLJ 7 & Up

Annotation: In the 1970s, 14-year-old Billy, son of a Minnesota dairy farmer, has to deal with his rival, King, both on and off the baseball field, when he falls for Suzy. She is King's blonde-haired neighbor, and King thinks she is his girlfriend. Companion novel to *Farm Team* (Harper Collins, 1995) and *Striking Out* (HarperCollins, 1993).

Booktalk: Billy's attention is not on the Minnesota Twins baseball game, even though baseball is in his blood—he's one of the best pitchers around. What's warming his blood right now is the feel of Suzy's back leaning up against his knees as they sit in the bleachers. He experiences a whole new kind of sweat when she unbuttons the top two buttons of her blouse to cool herself off. Billy is so intent on looking at the tiny blonde hairs on the back of Suzy's neck that he doesn't even see the ball coming—the foul ball that he "catches" with his front teeth. "Love hurts" takes on a whole new meaning for Billy.

Weaver, Will, *Striking Out.* 139

HarperTrophy, 1995, 296pp. $4.95. ISBN: 0-06-447113-6
Subjects: Baseball, Fathers and Sons
Genre: Sports
List: Author's Choice
Level: K 7–10

Annotations: Thirteen-year-old Billy Baggs has had a distant relationship with his father, a Minnesota dairy farmer, since his brother was killed five years before in a farm accident. When the coach of the town baseball team sees how Billy can pitch, Billy has something to do besides farm work.

Booktalk: Did you ever think about what farm or ranch kids do when they aren't in school? Billy Baggs lives on a dairy farm in northern Minnesota. When he isn't on the pitching mound throwing fast balls, he is working with his father. Guys, I am sure you will wince over some of the things Billy has to do on a dairy farm. Imagine being up at 4 a.m., trying to hold down a squirmy 8-week-old, 150-pound bull as your father takes a sharp little knife out of a bucket of soapy water, makes a quick cut, and then squeezes the testicles out in a bucket. By the end of the day, that bucket is full, and Billy carries it up to the barn loft and dumps the contents out for the cats to munch on. Life on a dairy farm is not easy for males of any species! No wonder Billy prefers to be on a pitching mound than working on the farm with his dad.

140 White, Ellen Emerson, *The Road Home.*

Scholastic, 1995, 464pp. $15.95. ISBN: 0-590-46737-9. Scholastic, 1995, $4.99. ISBN: 0-590-46738-7
Subjects: Emotional Problems, Occupations, Physically Handicapped, Vietnam War, War
Genre: Historical
Lists: 1998 PP, 1996 BBYA
Levels: BL 8–12, SLJ 8–12

Annotation: Twenty-two-year old Rebecca Phillips spent a grueling tour of duty as a front line nurse in Vietnam, but the war continues to haunt her. After she returns to the States, she cannot settle into civilian life. So she travels from Boston to Golden, Colorado, to find herself and the young soldier she fell in love with while in Vietnam. (Rebecca is a secondary character in the *Echo Company* series, which White wrote under the name of Zack White. The series is currently out of print.)

Booktalk: It was Christmas time and the Tet truce had turned into a major offensive. Rebecca had been working for over 48 hours straight. She was working on medical autopilot as she started IVs, and cut off legs and arms that were dangling by tendons. All of this was to save the surgeons time. And all of this was being done on a broken ankle because Rebecca's cast had split apart from the hectic pace. Since there was no time for a new one, she taped up her ankle during a few spare seconds and slipped her foot into the smallest boot she could find on the pile of cut-off limbs, after shaking a soldier's bloody foot out of it.

Curriculum Connection: History
Women have had a role in every war the United States has been involved in, but the Vietnam Conflict brought women closer to the front lines than any other war had. Have students do research on the nurses who did tours of duty in Vietnam and how this experience affected their lives when they returned to the United States.

141 Whitney, P. L., *This Is Graceanne's Book.*

St. Martin's Press, 1999, 298pp. $22.95. ISBN: 0-312-20597-X. Griffin Trade Paperback, 2001, 304pp. $13.95. ISBN: 0-312-27278-2
Subjects: Authorship, Brothers and Sisters, Child Abuse, Divorce, Family Problems, Mothers and Daughters, Race Relations
Genre: Historical
List: Author's Choice
Level: Adult

Annotation: During the 1960s in Missouri, nine-year-old Charlie narrates what life is like for his 12-year-old sister, Graceanne, the only one of the three children in his family whom their mother physically abuses. Feisty Graceanne will not allow her mother to break her spirit no matter how badly she beats her.

Booktalk: Life for Graceanne hadn't been easy when they lived on the base with their father. But when her parents divorced, it got much worse. Her mother, Edie, had grand plans for her life, but they sure weren't going to happen now that they were so poor they had to move into the black part of town. Whenever things didn't go right for Edie, she took them out on Graceanne, sometimes with a coat hanger, sometimes just with her hand. And things certainly weren't going right after they had moved. But no matter how hard Edie beat Graceanne, she couldn't break her daughter's spirit, and that made her angrier than anything else. The question was: How far would Edie go to break Graceanne?

142

Williams, Lori Aurelia, *When Kambia Elaine Flew in from Neptune.*

Simon & Schuster, 2000, 246pp. $17. ISBN: 0-689-82468-8. Aladdin, 2001, 246pp. $10. ISBN: 0-689-84593-6
Subjects: African Americans, Authorship, Child Sexual Abuse, Mothers and Daughters, Pregnancy, Sisters
Genres: Multicultural, Realistic
List: 2001 BBYA
Levels: BL 7–12, SLJ 8 & Up

Annotation: Twelve-year-old African-American Shayla has a wild 15-year-old sister, Tia, who has run away. Her father has moved back in to live with them in their Houston home. Her friend Kambia, a victim of sexual abuse, keeps getting thinner and thinner. Companion to *Shayla's Double Brown Baby Blues* (Simon & Schuster, 2001).

Booktalk: Shayla loves to write a good story, but her friend Kambia Elaine can tell stories so weird that Shayla doesn't even know what to think of them. Sometimes they are funny stories, such as how memory beetles fly to Earth from the dark side of Uranus and gather up the wonderful thoughts people don't want to forget. The memory beetles take them back to Uranus and store them in golden boxes in their caves until someone wants to remember them again. But when Kambia shakes in fear as she tells her about the Wallpaper Wolves, Shayla knows this isn't just a story—these wolves are real. Kambia needs help, but Shayla has promised not to tell anyone about the Wallpaper Wolves. But as Kambia keeps getting thinner and thinner, Shayla is not sure she can keep her promise.

143. Williams-Garcia, Rita, *Like Sisters on the Homefront.*

Dutton, 1995, 165pp. $15.99. ISBN: 0-525-67465-9. Viking Penguin, 1998, 176pp. $5.99. ISBN: 0-14-038561-4
Subjects: African Americans, Family Problems, Pregnancy
Genres: Multicultural, Realistic
Lists: 1996 BBYA, 1996 QP, 1999 PP
Award: Coretta Scott King Honor
Levels: BL 8–12, SLJ 7 & Up

Annotation: After having an abortion, 14-year-old Gayle and her infant son from her first pregnancy are sent to live with her aunt and uncle, who is a minister, in Georgia. She learns how different life is in a small Southern town than in the inner-city projects. Gayle also learns about her family history from her great-grandmother.

Booktalk: Gayle could not believe her mother had actually done this to her. She bought her a one-way ticket to Georgia. When Gayle got off the plane, they were waiting for her: a stern-faced giant of an uncle, an aunt, and a big, gawky cousin in knee socks! They got in the car, and all Gayle could think about was why couldn't they live in a city like Atlanta, at least. Her uncle just kept driving, past where any city bus would go, past where the highway ended, and onto a small road. Gayle watched the rows of oak and pine trees that lined the road on both sides. She grinned to herself as she saw the DEER CROSSING signs and the signs posted with hunting regulations. She couldn't help but think that putting up signs like that was what they should do back home in South Jamaica, New York. But these signs would say, "PLEASE DON'T SHOOT THE PEOPLE." City girl Gayle was about to experience culture shock, big time.

Curriculum Connections: English, History

When the main character, Gayle, moves to Georgia, she meets her great-grandmother, who is the matriarch of her family and the holder of the family history. Gayle did not have any knowledge of her extended family because her mother had moved away many years before. She did not have a strong concept of what family means. Have students discuss the concept of a family history and how they could go about creating one for themselves. Who in their immediate or extended family would be considered the holder of their family history? How far back could they go with this history? What major events in history come up when family members are asked about the past?

Wittlinger, Ellen, **Hard Love.**

Simon & Schuster, 1999, 224pp. $16.95. ISBN 0-689-82134-4. Aladdin 2001, 240pp. $8. ISBN: 0-689-84154-X

Subjects: Authorship, Divorce, Friendship, Homosexuality
Genre: Realistic
Lists: 2000 BBYA, 2000 QP
Award: Michael L. Printz Honor
Levels: BL 7–12, SLJ 7 & Up

144

Annotation: Sixteen-year-old lonely writer John meets his favorite zine author, Marisol. They become friends, but problems arise in their friendship when he falls in love with this vocally "out" Puerto Rican lesbian.

Booktalk: It's bad enough that I am normally in neutral when it comes to girls, but then, when I do fall for one, she is a Puerto Rican lesbian with black hair so spiky on the ends you would swear it could pierce your heart. I didn't know my heart was going to get involved. I honestly had no intention of falling in love. All I wanted to do was meet her, the writer of *Escape Velocity,* the zine I picked up at Tower Records. Our friendship was going fine until I was stupid enough to invite her to the prom and then forgot the ground rules. How could I help but not try to kiss her when she felt so good in my arms? Big mistake!

Curriculum Connection: English
   Divide students into groups of five. Each group researches zines, collecting as many as they can find in print or online. Each group designs its own zine to share with the rest of the class, writing about topics and issues important to them.

Wolff, Virginia Euwer, **True Believer.**

Atheneum 2001, 264pp. $17. ISBN: 0-689-82827-6

Subjects: Friendship, Homosexuality, Mothers and Daughters, Religion, Swimming
Genre: Realistic
List: 2002 BBYA
Levels: BL 7–12, SLJ 6 & Up

145

Annotation: Fifteen-year-old LaVaugh becomes infatuated with Jody, a childhood friend who returns to her school. She cannot share how she feels with her two best friends when she finds out Jody is gay, because they have become actively involved with a strict religious group in the area. Their friendship is already strained; they think she is uppity because she is taking classes to help her get into college. Companion novel to *Make Lemonade* (Holt, 1993).

Booktalk: LaVaugh can barely breathe every time she detects the slight smell of chlorine in the elevator of her apartment building or in the hallways at school. It isn't because she doesn't like the smell of chlorine, it is because she loves the source of the smell, her childhood friend Jody, a swimmer, who has returned to live downstairs from her. When she senses Jody's presence, her chest tightens up and she forgets how to talk. When he gets into the elevator with her, all she can do is stare and respond with garbled words to his hello. She writes his name on her biology notebook, and her lab partner asks which Jody is her boyfriend. When she says him, Jody the swimmer, he tells her it can't be that one. She doesn't understand why it truly cannot be "that one" until it is too late to stop her heart from breaking.

Curriculum Connection: English
This novel is written in free verse. Have students discuss whether this style of writing is easier or more difficult to read than the typical narrative style of writing.

146 Woodson, Jacqueline, *If You Come Softly.*

Putnam, 1998, 181pp. $15.99. ISBN: 0-399-23112-9. Penguin Putnam, 2000, 192pp. $4.99. ISBN: 0-698-11862-6
Subjects: African Americans, Death, Divorce, Jewish Americans, Race Relations, Relationships
Genres: Multicultural, Realistic
Lists: 2002 PP, 2000 B of BBYA, 1999 BBYA
Levels: BL 7–10, SLJ 7 & Up

Annotation: Fifteen-year-old private school students in New York City, Ellie and Jeremiah fall in love even though they know a relationship between a Jewish girl and a black boy is frowned upon. Jeremiah's divorced parents have accepted their relationship, but before Ellie can tell her parents, Jeremiah is shot by the police while running through the park in her white neighborhood.

Booktalk: Ellie and Jeremiah are very much in love, so much so that they spend every minute they can together. Jeremiah lives in Brooklyn, and Ellie lives uptown. They tolerate the stares of strangers as they walk hand in hand through the park to spend wonderful hours together in his mother's Brooklyn loft. Jeremiah knows Ellie's family will not be as supportive of their relationship as his is, so when she puts her Star of David around his neck and tells him he will get to meet them soon, Jeremiah is so excited he forgets his father's childhood warning—never run in a white man's neighborhood.

Curriculum Connection: Psychology
Biracial relationships make some people uncomfortable. Write an essay discussing whether you think biracial dating is acceptable, justifying your stand on this controversial issue.

147

Yee, Paul, *Breakaway.*

Publishing Group West, 1997, 144pp. $14.95. ISBN: 0-88899-289-0. Groundwood Books, 2000, 144pp. $5.95. ISBN: 0-88899-201-7

Subjects: Brothers and Sisters, Chinese, Fathers and Sons, Race Relations, Soccer
Genres: Historical, Multicultural, Sports
List: 1998 BBYA
Level: BL 7–12

Annotation: In 1932 in Vancouver, 18-year-old Kwok is first-generation Chinese-Canadian and experiences prejudice at school as well as on the soccer field. After realizing he will not receive a soccer scholarship because he is Chinese, Kwok joins the Chinese community's soccer team, and decides to stay and help his father on the farm.

Booktalk: Kwok's family did not live in Chinatown like most of the other Chinese families in the Vancouver area. Kwok's family lived on a pig farm in the country. He was trying to fit in with the other kids in his rural school, but being the only Chinese student in school, Kwok experienced prejudice and ridicule on a daily basis. What noise does a Chinese duck make? Kwok-kwok-kwok. Kwok had heard it all, either in the hallways or on the soccer field. He was bound and determined to get off the farm by getting a soccer scholarship to the university. Until then, swallowing his pride, Kwok went into Chinatown with his father and picked up the putrid slop buckets from the restaurants, free food for their pigs. But he would do this disgusting job only until his scholarship came through— and that had better be soon.

Curriculum Connection: History

This book is set in Vancouver, Canada, during the 1930s, the Depression era. Have students research the Depression in relation to other countries. Was the United States the only country suffering from lack of jobs and money?

148

Yolen, Jane, and Bruce Coville, *Armageddon Summer.*

Harcourt Brace, 1998, 272pp. $17. ISBN: 0-15-201767-4. Harcourt Brace, 1999, 266pp. $5.99. ISBN: 0-15-202268-6

Subjects: Family Problems, Friendship, Religion
Genre: Realistic
List: 1999 BBYA, 1999 QP
Levels: BL 7–12, SLJ 6–8

Annotation: The mother of 14-year-old Marina and the father of 16-year-old Jed take the teens with them to join Reverend Beelson's Believers in a remote compound built on top of a mountain, waiting for the end of the world.

Booktalk: Marina wanted to believe Reverend Beelson. But the idea of fires burning, seas overflowing, and the wicked drowning in their own blood with only the Believers safe on their mountaintop seemed a bit much. July 27, Marina's 14th birthday, was to be the Day of Armageddon. At the service that night, Marina didn't shout "Amen!" loudly with the rest of the Believers. She knew God could hear her whether she whispered or shouted. She also knew He knew that she was not entirely sure she wanted to be saved, not without her dad, who was not a Believer. What Marina didn't know was that she would soon meet Jed, who was as skeptical as she was about this whole idea of Armageddon.

Curriculum Connection: History

The end of the world has been predicted throughout the centuries. Have students research the past threats of Armageddon. What has been occurring in the world for an end-of-the-world prediction to arise during each of the researched time periods?

149 Zindel, Paul, *Reef of Death.*

HarperCollins, 1998, 177pp. $15.89. ISBN: 0-06-024733-9. Disney Press, 1999, 192pp. $5.99. ISBN: 0-7868-1408-X
Subjects: Brothers and Sisters, Death
Genres: Horror, Multicultural, Mystery
Lists: 2000 YAC, 1999 QP
Levels: BL 7–12, SLJ 6–9

Annotation: Set on Australia's Great Barrier Reef, this book tells the story of how 17-year-old PC helps an aboriginal girl find a missing sacred treasure, and encounters a sadistic scientist and the undersea monster that killed the girl's brother.

Booktalk: Arnhem and his sister, Maruul, were searching for the sacred treasure in the cliffs of the Great Barrier Reef when they heard a mechanical scream. Maruul looked down into the water, searching for her brother, knowing it was time for him to surface. That's when she saw the huge fishlike creature rising out of the ocean's depths, its cavernous mouth filled with razor-sharp teeth. It was rising toward the surface at a speed that belied its size. That is all she remembered. They later found Maruul curled up in the bottom of the kayak, still screaming. They never did find Arnhem, her brother.

Zusak, Markus, *Fighting Ruben Wolfe.*

Scholastic, 2001, 224pp. $15.95. ISBN: 0-439-24188-X
Subjects: Boxing, Brothers, Family Problems
Genre: Sports
List: 2002 BBYA
Levels: BL 8–12, SLJ 7 & Up

Annotation: Two teenage brothers from a close-knit, working-class Australian family begin boxing for a sleazy promoter. They discover they are fighting for more than the payoff money—they are fighting for their pride.

Booktalk: Cameron and Rube Wolfe know that their sister, Sarah, comes in drunk most nights. They also know she has been running around. But no one else better say anything about it. Rube lets the taunts about his unemployed father roll off his back as he walks down the school hallway. He doesn't react until the dumb bloke makes a derogatory comment about Sarah. Cameron shouts "Rube!" but his older brother has already bloodied his knuckles on the guy's teeth. Rube keeps hammering him with his fists until the guy's legs buckle and he hits the floor. Rube is as surprised as everyone else who saw what happened. Cameron and Rube had sparred in the backyard with boxing gloves, but he didn't know he was that good. The difference? This time it is for real. Nobody is going to get away with talking about his sister like that—nobody.

SECTION 6

Indexes

For ease of access, the numbers in the indexes refer to the entry number, rather than to a page number.

A. Author

Abelove, Joan, *Saying It Out Loud*	1
Alder, Elizabeth, *The King's Shadow*	2
Anderson, Laurie Halse, *Fever 1793*	3
Anderson, Laurie Halse, *Speak*	4
Atkins, Catherine, *When Jeff Comes Home*	5
Atwater-Rhodes, Amelia, *In the Forests of the Night*	6
Bauer, Joan, *Rules of the Road*	7
Bauer, Joan, *Thwonk*	8
Bennett, Cherie, *Life in the Fat Lane*	9
Block, Francesca Lia, *Baby Be-Bop*	10
Block, Francesca Lia, *I Was a Teenage Fairy*	11
Block, Francesca Lia, *Violet & Claire*	12
Blume, Judy, *Forever*	13
Brooks, Terry, *Magic Kingdom for Sale: Sold!*	14
Burgess, Melvin, *Smack*	15
Cadnum, Michael, *Rundown*	16

Carter, Alden R., *Between a Rock and a Hard Place* 17
Carter, Alden R., *Up Country* 18
Cascone, A. G., *If He Hollers* 19
Chbosky, Stephen, *The Perks of Being a Wildflower* 20
Cochran, Thomas, *Roughnecks* 21
Conford, Ellen, *Crush* 22
Cook, Karin, *What Girls Learn* 23
Cooney, Caroline B., *Both Sides of Time* 24
Cooney, Caroline B., *Driver's Ed* 25
Cooney, Caroline B., *The Terrorist* 26
Cooney, Caroline B., *Voice on the Radio* 27
Cormier, Robert, *Heroes* 28
Cormier, Robert, *In the Middle of the Night* 29
Cross, Gillian, *Tightrope* 30
Crutcher, Chris, *Ironman* 31
Crutcher, Chris, *Staying Fat for Sarah Byrnes* 32
Dickinson, Peter, *Eva* 33
Draper, Sharon, *Darkness Before Dawn* 34
Draper, Sharon, *Forged by Fire* 35
Draper, Sharon, *Tears of a Tiger* 36
Duncan, Lois, *I Know What You Did Last Summer* 37
Ferris, Jean, *Love Among the Walnuts* 38
Fleischman, Paul, *Mind's Eye* 39
Fraustino, Lisa Rowe, *Ash* 40
French, Albert, *Billy* 41
Gilbert, Barbara Snow, *Stone Water* 42
Gilstrap, John, *Nathan's Run* 43
Glovach, Linda, *Beauty Queen* 44
Goldman, E. M., *Getting Lincoln's Goat* 45
Grant, Cynthia D., *Mary Wolf* 46
Grant, Cynthia D., *The White Horse* 47
Grimes, Nikki, *Jazmin's Notebook* 48
Haddix, Margaret Peterson, *Don't You Dare Read This, Mrs. Dunphrey* 49
Haddix, Margaret Peterson, *Turnabout* 50
Hahn, Mary Downing, *The Wind Blows Backward* 51
Hanauer, Cathi, *My Sister's Bones* 52
Hardman, Ric Lynden, *Sunshine Rider: The First Vegetarian Western* 53
Hautman, Pete, *Mr. Was* 54
Hautman, Pete, *Stone Cold* 55
Henry, Chad, *DogBreath Victorious* 56
Hesser, Terry Spencer, *Kissing Doorknobs* 57
Hewett, Lorri, *Dancer* 58
Hewett, Lorri, *Lives of Our Own* 59
Hobbs, Valerie, *Get It While It's Hot. Or Not* 60
Hobbs, Valerie, *How Far Would You Have Gotten If I Hadn't Called You Back?* 61
Howe, James, *The Watcher* 62
Howe, Norma, *Adventures of Blue Avenger* 63
Howe, Norma, *Blue Avenger Cracks the Code* 64

Hurwin, Davida Wills, *Time for Dancing* 65
Huth, Angela, *Land Girls* 66
Jordan, Sherryl, *Raging Quiet* 67
Jordan, Sherryl, *Secret Sacrament* 68
Kerr, M. E., *Deliver Us from Evie* 69
Kerr, M. E., *"Hello," I Lied* 70
Klass, David, *California Blue* 71
Klass, David, *Danger Zone* 72
Klass, David, *Screen Test* 73
Klause, Annette Curtis, *Blood and Chocolate* 74
Klause, Annette Curtis, *Silver Kiss* 75
Krisher, Trudy, *Kinship* 76
Lane, Dakota, *Johnny Voodoo* 77
Lee, Marie G., *Necessary Roughness* 78
Lester, Julius, *Othello: A Novel* 79
Levenkron, Steven, *Luckiest Girl in the World* 80
Levitin, Sonia, *The Cure* 81
Logue, Mary, *Dancing with an Alien* 82
Lynch, Chris, *Extreme Elvin* 83
Lynch, Chris, *Iceman* 84
Lynch, Chris, *Slot Machine* 85
Lynch, Chris, *Whitechurch* 86
Marchetta, Melina, *Looking for Alibrandi* 87
Marsden, John, *Tomorrow When the War Began* 88
Martinez, Victor, *Parrot in the Oven* 89
Mazer, Norma Fox, *Out of Control* 90
Mazer, Norma Fox, *When She Was Good* 91
McCants, William D., *Much Ado About Prom Night* 92
McDonald, Joyce, *Swallowing Stones* 93
Meyer, Carolyn, *Drummers of Jericho* 94
Moore, Martha, *Angels on the Roof* 95
Mori, Kyoko, *One Bird* 96
Morressy, John, *Juggler* 97
Myers, Walter Dean, *Fallen Angels* 98
Myers, Walter Dean, *Monster* 99
Myers, Walter Dean, *Slam!* 100
Namioka, Lensey, *Ties That Bind, Ties That Break* 101
Napoli, Donna Jo, *Beast* 102
Nix, Garth, *Sabriel* 103
Nix, Garth, *Shade's Children* 104
Nixon, Joan Lowery, *The Haunting* 105
Nolan, Han, *Dancing on the Edge* 106
Orr, Wendy, *Peeling the Onion* 107
Paulsen, Gary, *Sarny: A Life Remembered* 108
Paulsen, Gary, *Soldier's Heart* 109
Peck, Richard, *Last Safe Place on Earth* 110
Powell, Randy, *Dean Duffy* 111
Preston, Douglas, and Lincoln Child, *The Relic* 112

Qualey, Marsha, *Come in from the Cold* 113
Randle, Kristen D., *The Only Alien on the Planet* 114
Reuter, Bjarne, *The Boys from St. Petri* 115
Rosenberg, Joel, *Not Exactly the Three Musketeers* 116
Seymour, Tres, *The Revelation of St. Bruce* 117
Shoup, Barbara, *Stranded in Harmony* 118
Shusterman, Neal, *Downsiders* 119
Sleator William, *House of Stairs* 120
Soto, Gary, *Buried Onions* 121
Stoehr, Shelly, *Tomorrow Wendy: A Love Story* 122
Strasser, Todd, *Give a Boy a Gun* 123
Sweeney, Joyce, *Free Fall* 124
Sweeney, Joyce, *Spirit Window* 125
Sykes, Shelley, *For Mike* 126
Taylor, Theodore, *The Bomb* 127
Temple, Frances, *The Ramsay Scallop* 128
Thesman, Jean, *The Moonstone* 129
Thomas, Rob, *Rats Saw God* 130
Thompson, Julian F., *The Grounding of Group 6* 131
Van Dijik, Lutz, *Damned Strong Love: The True Story of Willi G. and Stephan K.* 132
Vande Velde, Vivian, *Companions of the Night* 133
Vande Velde, Vivian, *Never Trust a Dead Man* 134
Voigt, Cynthia, *When She Hollers* 135
Wallace, Rich, *Wrestling Sturbridge* 136
Weaver, Will, *Farm Team* 137
Weaver, Will, *Hard Ball* 138
Weaver, Will, *Striking Out* 139
White, Ellen Emerson, *The Road Home* 140
Whitney, P. L., *This Is GraceAnne's Book* 141
Williams, Lori Aurelia, *When Kambia Elaine Flew in from Neptune* 142
Williams-Garcia, Rita, *Like Sisters on the Homefront* 143
Wittlinger, Ellen, *Hard Love* 144
Wolff, Virginia Euwer, *True Believer* 145
Woodson, Jacqueline, *If You Come Softly* 146
Yee, Paul, *Breakaway* 147
Yolen, Jane, and Bruce Coville, *Armageddon Summer* 148
Zindel, Paul, *Reef of Death* 149
Zusak, Markus, *Fighting Ruben Wolfe* 150

B. Title

Adventures of Blue Avenger, Howe 63
Angels on the Roof, Moore..95
Armageddon Summer, Yolen 148
Ash, Fraustino 40
Baby Be-Bop, Block 10
Beast, Napoli 102

Beauty Queen, Glovach 44
Between a Rock and a Hard Place, Carter 17
Billy, French 41
Blood and Chocolate, Klause 74
Blue Avenger Cracks the Code, Howe 64
The Bomb, Taylor 127
Both Sides of Time, Cooney 24
The Boys from St. Petri, Reuter 115
Breakaway, Yee 147
Buried Onions, Soto 121
California Blue, Klass 71
Come in from the Cold, Qualey 113
Companions of the Night, Vande Velde 133
Crush, Conford 22
The Cure, Levitin 81
Damned Strong Love: The True Story of Willi G. and Stephan K., Van Dijik 132
Dancer, Hewett 58
Dancing on the Edge, Nolan 106
Dancing with an Alien, Logue 82
Danger Zone, Klass 72
Darkness Before Dawn, Draper 34
Dean Duffy, Powell 111
Deliver Us from Evie, Kerr 69
DogBreath Victorious, Henry 56
Don't You Dare Read This, Mrs. Dunphrey, Haddix 49
Downsiders, Shusterman 119
Driver's Ed, Cooney 25
Drummers of Jericho, Meyer 94
Eva, Dickinson 33
Extreme Elvin, Lynch 83
Fallen Angels, Myers 98
Farm Team, Weaver 137
Fever 1793, Anderson 3
Fighting Ruben Wolfe, Zusak 150
For Mike, Sykes 126
Forever, Blume 13
Forged by Fire, Draper 35
Free Fall, Sweeney 124
Get It While It's Hot. Or Not, Hobbs 60
Getting Lincoln's Goat, Goldman 45
Give a Boy a Gun, Strasser 123
Grounding of Group 6, The, Thompson 131
Hard Ball, Weaver 138
Hard Love, Wittlinger 144
The Haunting, Nixon 105
"Hello," I Lied," Kerr 70
Heroes, Cormier 28
House of Stairs, Sleator 120

How Far Would You Have Gotten If I Hadn't Called You Back?, Hobbs 61
I Know What You Did Last Summer, Duncan 37
I Was a Teenage Fairy, Block..........................11
Iceman, Lynch 84
If He Hollers, Cascone 19
If You Come Softly, Woodson 146
In the Forests of the Night, Atwater-Rhodes 6
In the Middle of the Night, Cormier 29
Ironman, Crutcher 31
Jazmin's Notebook, Grimes 48
Johnny Voodoo, Lane 77
Juggler, Morressy 97
The King's Shadow, Alder 2
Kinship, Krisher 76
Kissing Doorknobs, Hesser 57
Land Girls, Huth 66
Last Safe Place on Earth, Peck 110
Life in the Fat Lane, Bennett 9
Like Sisters on the Homefront, Williams-Garcia 143
Lives of Our Own, Hewett 59
Looking for Alibrandi, Marchetta 87
Love Among the Walnuts, Ferris 38
Luckiest Girl in the World, Levenkron 80
Magic Kingdom for Sale: Sold! Brooks 14
Mary Wolf, Grant 46
Mind's Eye, Fleischman 39
Monster, Myers 99
The Moonstones, Thesman 129
Mr. Was, Hautman 54
Much Ado About Prom Night, McCants 92
My Sister's Bones, Hanauer 52
Nathan's Run, Gilstrap 43
Necessary Roughness, Lee 78
Never Trust a Dead Man, Vande Velde 134
Not Exactly the Three Musketeers, Rosenberg 116
One Bird, Mori 96
The Only Alien on the Planet, Randle 114
Othello, A Novel, Lester 79
Out of Control, Mazer 90
Parrot in the Oven, Martinez 89
Peeling the Onion, Orr 107
The Perks of Being a Wildflower, Chbosky 20
Raging Quiet, Jordan 67
The Ramsay Scallop, Temple 128
Rats Saw God, Thomas 130
Reef of Death, Zindel 149
The Relic, Preston 112
The Revelation of St. Bruce, Seymour 117

Roughnecks, Cochran	21
The Road Home, White	140
Rules of the Road, Bauer	7
Rundown, Cadnum	16
Sabriel, Nix	103
Sarny: A Life Remembered, Paulsen	108
Saying It Out Loud, Abelove	1
Screen Test, Klass	73
Secret Sacrament, Jordan	68
Shade's Children, Nix	104
Silver Kiss, Klause	75
Slam!, Myers	100
Slot Machine, Lynch	85
Smack, Burgess	15
Soldier's Heart, Paulsen	109
Speak, Anderson	4
Spirit Window, Sweeney	125
Staying Fat for Sarah Byrnes, Crutcher	32
Stone Cold, Hautman	55
Stone Water, Gilbert	42
Stranded in Harmony, Shoup	118
Striking Out, Weaver	139
Sunshine Rider: The First Vegetarian Western, Hardman	53
Swallowing Stones, McDonald	93
Tears of a Tiger, Draper	36
The Terrorist, Cooney	26
This Is GraceAnne's Book, Whitney	141
Thwonk, Bauer	8
Ties That Bind, Ties That Break, Namioka	101
Tightrope, Cross	30
Time for Dancing, Hurwin	65
Tomorrow Wendy: A Love Story, Stoehr	122
Tomorrow When the War Began, Marsden	88
True Believer, Wolff	145
Turnabout, Haddix	50
Up Country, Carter	18
Violet & Claire, Block	12
Voice on the Radio, Cooney	27
The Watcher, Howe	62
What Girls Learn, Cook	23
When Jeff Comes Home, Atkins	5
When Kambia Elaine Flew in from Neptune, Williams	142
When She Hollers, Voigt	135
When She Was Good, Mazer	91
The White Horse, Grant	47
Whitechurch, Lynch	86
The Wind Blows Backward, Hahn	51
Wrestling Sturbridge, Wallace	136

C. Subject

Accidents	25, 29, 33, 36, 37, 107
African Americans	34, 35, 36, 41, 48, 58, 59, 72, 98, 99, 100, 108, 142, 143, 146
Alcoholism	7, 18, 89
Automobile Driving	7, 25, 61
Authorship	12, 36, 48, 60, 62, 64, 99, 130, 142, 144
Baseball	111, 137, 138, 139
Basketball	35, 36, 72, 100
Boxing	150
Brothers	37, 40, 75, 84, 98, 114, 115, 124, 150
Brothers and Sisters	6, 26, 27, 35, 49, 69, 76, 113, 133, 141, 147, 149
Camping	17, 88, 131
Cancer	1, 23, 65, 71, 75
Censorship	110
Child Abuse	32, 43, 49, 62, 91, 95, 114, 141
Child Sexual Abuse	5, 11, 20, 35, 135, 142
Chinese	101, 147
Civil War	108, 109
Dancing	58, 65
Death	1, 14, 19, 23, 25, 36, 42, 44, 46, 61, 63, 65, 75, 77, 79, 81, 86, 93, 98, 103, 121, 124, 125, 126, 127, 146, 149
Devil, the	97
Diabetes	17
Divorce	96, 141, 144, 146
Dragons	14, 116
Drug Abuse	15, 44, 47, 122, 130
Eating Disorders	9, 52
Ecology	71, 125, 127
Elderly, the	7, 38, 39, 42, 50, 118
Emotional Problems	4, 20, 51, 80, 91, 107, 140
Epidemics	3, 81
Extraterrestrial Beings	82, 104
Fairies	11, 102
Family Problems	9, 18, 30, 40, 46, 47, 54, 55, 57, 62, 76, 77, 89, 91, 95, 101, 121, 129, 141, 143, 148, 150
Fathers and Daughters	1, 32, 46, 49, 52, 76, 77, 87, 101, 102, 103, 106, 125
Fathers and Sons	5, 17, 31, 51, 63, 68, 71, 78, 99, 130, 137, 138, 139, 147
Figure Skating	80
Football	21, 31, 78, 118
Friendship	12, 27, 31, 32, 37, 50, 57, 60, 65, 66, 70, 79, 82, 83, 85, 86, 88, 93, 98, 104, 114, 116, 117, 118, 119, 120, 124, 126, 127, 131, 136, 137, 138, 144, 145, 148
Gambling	55, 131
Gangs	30, 89, 115, 121
Ghosts	10, 105, 126
Grandparents	3, 10, 42, 54, 106, 125, 127
High Schools	4, 8, 9, 20, 22, 25, 26, 31, 32, 34, 36, 45, 59, 63, 64, 77, 83, 87, 90, 92, 94, 100, 110, 117, 123, 130

Hockey	84
Homosexuality	10, 69, 70, 122, 132, 144, 145
Japanese	96
Jewish Americans	1, 52, 94, 146
Jews	81, 132
Journal Writing	44, 48, 49, 99
Kidnapping	5, 19, 27, 133
Kings	2, 14
Korean Americans	78
Letter Writing	20, 31, 36, 40, 56, 85
Magic	14, 68, 97, 102, 103, 116
Medical Experimentation	33, 50, 82, 104, 120
Mental Illness	19, 29, 38, 40, 57, 80, 86, 91, 106, 109, 114, 122
Mexican Americans	89, 121
Middle Ages	2, 81, 97, 128
Mothers and Daughters	3, 11, 23, 30, 47, 48, 60, 76, 80, 87, 95, 96, 129, 141, 142, 145
Mothers and Sons	56, 83, 85
Moving	9, 54, 61, 77, 78, 95
Murder	26, 37, 41, 43, 54, 79, 86, 99, 105, 112, 134
Music	56, 61, 70, 77, 81, 94, 122
Occupations	45, 53, 68, 69, 73, 96, 140
Old West, the	53
Parent and Child	16, 27, 33, 38, 84, 105, 108, 131
Photography	8, 125
Physically Handicapped	2, 28, 29, 39, 67, 107, 140
Pregnancy	15, 47, 60, 82, 87, 142, 143
Race Relations	1, 3, 41, 58, 59, 68, 72, 77, 78, 79, 81, 94, 98, 141, 146, 147
Rape	4, 16, 28, 34
Relationships	8, 21, 22, 24, 51, 61, 63, 66, 67, 68, 73, 74, 75, 77, 79, 82, 83, 87, 92, 97, 110, 113, 128, 146
Religion	110, 117, 126, 128, 145, 148
Self-esteem	5, 14, 16, 20, 21, 53, 101, 103, 111, 120, 123, 135, 136
Sexual Assault	90
Sexual Relationships	13, 52, 70, 118, 122
Sisters	16, 23, 48, 52, 91, 142
Slavery	2, 108
Soccer,	147
Stepfamilies	23, 35, 94, 135
Suicide	28, 36, 42, 51, 61, 123
Survival	17, 33, 88, 119, 124, 131
Swimming	32, 82, 145
Teachers	47, 49, 108
Terrorism	26
Time Travel	6, 24, 54, 81
Track and Field	16, 34, 71
Vampires	6, 75, 133
Viewnam War	98, 113, 140

Vietnam War Protests 113, 118
Violence 98, 121, 123
War 28, 54, 66, 88, 98, 104, 108, 109, 115, 132, 140
Weight Control 9, 32, 83, 85
Werewolves 74
Witchcraft 67, 134
World War II 28, 54, 66, 115, 132
Wrestling 85, 136

D. Genre

Adventure 17, 88, 124, 131
Fantasy 11, 14, 54, 68, 102, 103, 116
Historical 2, 3, 23, 24, 28, 41, 48, 53, 54, 61, 66, 67, 79, 81, 97, 98, 101, 108, 109, 113, 115, 127, 128, 132, 140, 141, 147
Horror 6, 19, 74, 75, 97, 112, 131, 133, 149
Humor 7, 8, 22, 38, 45, 53, 56, 63, 64, 83, 85, 92, 134
Multicultural 1, 34, 35, 36, 41, 48, 52, 58, 59, 68, 72, 77, 78, 79, 81, 87, 89, 94, 96, 98, 99, 100, 101, 102, 108, 121, 125, 127, 132, 142, 143, 146, 147, 149
Mystery 19, 26, 29, 30, 37, 38, 43, 45, 54, 64, 105, 112, 126, 134, 149
Realistic 1, 4, 5, 7, 9, 10, 11, 12, 13, 15, 16, 18, 20, 25, 26, 27, 29, 30, 31, 32, 34, 35, 36, 37, 39, 40, 42, 43, 44, 46, 47, 49, 51, 52, 55, 57, 58, 59, 60, 62, 63, 64, 65, 69, 70, 71, 73, 76, 77, 78, 80, 83, 84, 86, 87, 89, 90, 91, 92, 93, 94, 95, 99, 100, 106, 107, 110, 111, 114, 117, 118, 121, 122, 123, 124, 125, 129, 130, 135, 142, 143, 144, 145, 146, 148
Romance 8, 13, 22, 24, 51, 61, 67, 68, 73, 74, 75, 77, 79, 82
Science Fiction 33, 50, 81, 82, 104, 113, 119, 120
Sports ..16, 21, 31, 32, 71, 72, 78, 80, 84, 85, 100, 111, 136, 137, 138, 139, 147, 150
Supernatural 6, 10, 24, 75, 105, 125, 126, 134

E. Curriculum Connections

Art 95
Career Education 45, 52, 61, 69, 73
English 1, 4, 6, 8, 20, 22, 36, 37, 39, 48, 51, 52, 62, 64, 75, 79, 82, 93, 97, 99, 100, 102, 105, 110, 116, 117, 124, 143, 144, 145
Government 26, 27, 33, 34, 41, 43, 94, 117
Health 3, 9, 13, 17, 23, 31, 40, 42, 44, 50, 53, 57, 60, 65, 80, 83, 90, 106
History 2, 3, 24, 26, 28, 41, 54, 58, 59, 66, 67, 81, 87, 88, 98, 101, 108, 109, 110, 113, 115, 118, 119, 127, 128, 129, 132, 140, 143, 147, 148
Math 78, 96
Physical Education 31, 72, 84, 85, 107, 111
Psychology 20, 22, 23, 25, 27, 34, 36, 40, 42, 46, 50, 52, 55, 57, 63, 72, 76, 80, 90, 92, 94, 96, 99, 100, 106, 120, 123, 124, 126, 146
Science 14, 33, 71, 125
Sociology 30, 46, 78, 87, 94, 101, 119, 123, 137